BENSENVILLE

MARTHA KIRKER JONES

Village of Bensenville, Illinois

The Commission specially thanks Roger Ewert for his technical editing, Wilma Reges for transcribing the oral history tape recordings, and Darleen Kral for her many suggestions, competent assistance and attention to detail.

BENSENVILLE BICENTENNIAL COMMISSION

Wilbur Burde and Rev. Erling Jacobson—Co-chairmen

Frank Bartolone
Lucy Benziger
James Coad
Richard Delventhal
Richard Franzen
Martha Jones
Kenneth Kaufman
George Korthauer, Jr.
Darleen Kral

Litzie Leider
Kay Lorden
John Martens
Lillian Mueller
Oliver Patterson
Lorry Schlichting
Clifford Sell
Elsie Todd

The Bensenville Bicentennial Commission is particularly grateful to the following people who have shared their records, recollections, time, traditions, photographs, and diaries to create an account of past events.

Mr. and Mrs. Victor Barth
Rev. E. Bergstraesser
Mrs. Ida Boeske
William Bourke
Sid Ceaser
Violet Christensen
Churchville Historical Society
Philip Clark
Ethel Dehlinger
Frank DeVita
Herbert Dierking
Mr. and Mrs. Charles Earhart
Lucille Eichinger
Mr. and Mrs. Chester Franzen
Richard Franzen
Mrs. Irving O. Geils
Leonard Geils
Mrs. Erna Hackmeister
Mr. and Mrs. William Hegebarth
Martin Heinrich
Mrs. Katie Howell
Jean Johnson
Mr. and Mrs. Wesley A. Johnson
Scott Kinnaman
Armin Korthauer
Mrs. George L. Korthauer, Sr.
John Kral
Mr. and Mrs. Les Lange
Lillie Lange
Litzie Leider
Carol Livingston
Mr. and Mrs. Martin Luessenhop
Mr. and Mrs. Fred Mueller
Virginia Northrop
Mr. and Mrs. Walter Olhaber
Charles Ortega
Holly Ekstrom

Sue Pera
Harold Pfluger
Thomas Phillips
Dan Plaza
Conway Ramseyer
Edgar Rapin
Miss Alvina Rittmueller
Martin Romme
Mrs. A. F. Rosenwinkle
Russell Roth
Mr. and Mrs. Marvin Rusteberg
John Schoo
Willard Schoppe
Marie Sievert
Mrs. Henry Senne
Sgt. Robert Schneider
Paula Sinclair
Mr. and Mrs. Francis Suter
Walter Tett
Virginia Thomas
Mr. and Mrs. Gust Van Mol
Fred Valentino
Marge Varble
Lee Vick
Miss Cora Warnecke
Dorothy Dean Weir
Evelyn Wilkinson
Richard Weber
Bernice Wolf
Bensenville Community Public
    Library
Bensenville Park District
Veterans of Foreign Wars
    Post 2149
Veterans of Foreign Wars
    Post 2149 Auxillary
Village of Bensenville

It has been said that remembrance is a form of meeting, and it is hoped that these remembrances of a village's beginnings and growth will allow us to meet individuals, events, and ways of living which created the town we live in. Bensenville was created by a group of people who used the resources of mind and land available, first building with their own hands houses, farms, schools, and churches, and then organizing a local government to serve the needs of the community. They invented, improvised, coped, and endured. A shared knowledge of the community's past contributes to a sense of unity and belonging. We would remember our past for the strength and joy it brings to the present.

Martha Kirker Jones

THE VILLAGE

"About the first or second day of April, 1884, several citizens and residents of Bensenville, in ordinary conversation, brought up the question if it would not benefit the village to have it incorporated"...so begins the village record. The two square miles of territory cited in the petition to County Court Judge Elbert H. Gary for incorporation had 325 inhabitants. The location of the village was considered by a contemporary writer to be beautiful and healthful. It was thought incorporation might be, "the simplest and best way to settle the pending school question." The village children walked two miles south to the one-room school at Churchville on Church Road, or north to a school at York Road and Thorndale, struggling through a slough known as the Black Sea in wet weather. Farms were a part of the village, and it was necessary to have these farmers become part of the corporate limits in order to meet the legal population requirements.

"It was agreed Herman H. Korthauer should devise ways and means to find out the opinion of the majority of the residents," and determine the requirements and procedures for incorporation. Herman H. Korthauer was to spend the rest of his long life devising ways and means for the Village of Bensenville. As the oldest son of an early settler, he was one of a generation of Addison Township men who would lay the foundation of civic organization and government in this area. He posted notices for a meeting to be held April 5, 1884, at 7 p.m. at the Korthauer Hardware Store, "to find out the opinion of the residents."

Businesses and homes were established around Addison, Center, Green, and Elmhurst (York Road) Streets. A depot served the Chicago, Milwaukee, and St. Paul Railroad. There was the hardware store, a lumber and coal yard, a doctor, a stone mason, two grocery stores, a gristmill, blacksmiths, shoemakers, harness makers, a tinsmith, and carpenters. There was no school in the village and it was necessary to go south to Churchville or north to St. Johanne's for church services.

Herman H. Korthauer called the meeting to order and explained the reason for the meeting. Henry Korthauer was selected chairman, and C. A. Franzen was selected to act as clerk. "Then Mr. Henry Korthauer explained more explicitly and minutely the subject of the meeting," if it would benefit Bensenville to be organized under the general laws of the state. The question was held for debate, and it was decided to appoint a committee of six to investigate incorporation, draw an agreement with surrounding farmers, settle a boundary line, determine the percentage over which taxable property could not be assessed for corporate purposes, and draw the petition to be presented to the county judge to fix a day for election for or against organization. This committee included: Henry Korthauer, 62, farmer, carpenter, and nurseryman; John H. Franzen, 71, farmer and flaxmill owner; August Schwardtfeger, 39, farmer; George Cogswell, 37, farmer; Henry Cogswell, 32, former machinery salesman; and Herman H. Korthauer, 32, hardware store owner, to act as clerk. Four other gentlemen, Frederick Eichhoff, Fred H. Tonne, Dietrich Kraegel Jr., and Christian Baucke were to ascertain the probable cost of a school building. The committees were to report one week later.

The following Saturday, April 12, Henry Korthauer called the meeting to order at the hardware store. The committee

Herman H. Korthauer's Hardware Store at Center and Main Street

Churchville School

3

on incorporation reported in favor of organization, defined the limits, agreed on a pledged resolution of disconnection, set the time limit at three years, and proposed a tax rate of twenty-five cents to one hundred dollars of taxable property. This report was accepted. The school committee reported that the probable cost of a school building large enough to accommodate fifty or sixty children would cost $1,300. This report was put on the table.

Thirty legal citizens mutually pledged themselves able to elect such men as trustees who would be representative, reliable, and trustworthy. It was agreed the trustees would serve without salary or fees and that the liquor or beer license money be kept by the corporation for the school fund. Proper notice was put up to have the election May 10, 1884.

Forty-nine handwritten ballots were cast in the vote for incorporation, forty-two to organize and seven against organization. As a result, an "election was ordered to be held at the store of Herman H. Korthauer in Bensenville commencing at 8 a.m. and closing at 7 in the evening for the purpose of electing officers of said village as provided by law." The results of the first election were that Henry Korthauer, Louis Schroeder, B. L. Franzen, George Cogswell, Christian Baucke, and Herman Korthauer received the largest number of votes and so constituted the first board of trustees. At their first meeting in the store on June 25, 1884, they drew ballots to determine terms of office, as half the board would serve the full two-year term and the other half would stand for election at the end of one year. Then they elected George Cogswell president of the village. Herman H. Korthauer was elected clerk and P. T. Tiedemann elected treasurer. Committees were appointed and Bensenville was in business.

INDIAN BACKGROUND

Bensenville's place names, Tioga, Blackhawk, Mohawk, and Chippewa, reflect DuPage County's Indian history. Old surveyors' plats of Bensenville have Tioga lettered above the crosshatching of the village's subdivision. A local legend calls Green Street an Indian trail. Many Bensenville children recall finding Indian artifacts in Fischer's pond at Church Road and Grand Avenue. In the 1600's the Illinois tribe lived in the area of present-day Bensenville, but their culture was disrupted by the development of the fur trade by the French trappers. The Illinois were driven west by a number of other Indian tribes, almost all of them Algonquians. The Saux, Foxes, Potawatomies, Ottawas, Menominees, Kickapoos, and Ojibwas occupied the land around Lake Michigan and Lake Superior. DuPage County has several known Potawatomi village sites. The two closest to Bensenville are the Churchill Forest Preserve and the bend of Salt Creek overlooking Oakbrook, two miles south of Elmhurst. Relics from chipping stations, where arrowheads were chipped from flint, are found in DuPage County also.

The Potawatomi were primarily a peaceful and sedentary tribe who built villages of long, bark-covered lodges and cultivated gardens of beans, squash, pumpkins, and corn. They moved periodically to hunt and fish. The rich black soil supported tall prairie grasses, clear creeks and rivers, and in Addison Township, a dense woodland of oak, hickory, walnut, and poplar trees. Bears, elk, deer, prairie chickens, quail, and wild turkeys could be hunted.

Although the Potawatomi had been the aggressors at the Fort Dearborn Massacre in 1812, they refused to join Black Hawk's uprising in 1832. They had lived peaceably for many years and had given the United States government no reason to demand their land. Their villages were loosely governed by chiefs and councils, although in times of war and danger, they were led by warriors who had gained followers by previous acts of leadership and valor. Family relationships were traced through the father, and men in villages were divided into groups that competed against each other in games and mock war raids. The world was believed to be filled with spirits that could give advice and help, and by fasting and solitary vigils, men sought the guardianship of a spirit in a dream or vision.

Illinois became a state in 1818, and by 1829, the United States government ordered the Saux and Fox to leave their lands in northwestern Illinois. Some tribes moved peaceably across the Mississippi into Iowa, but some stayed, and as the settlers moved in and plowed the land, disputes arose. The Indians, understandably reluctant to leave their land, threatened the settlers, who then appealed to the governor. A volunteer army marched against the Indians, who moved west. In 1832, Black Hawk, the Saux war chief, disputed the treaty and returned to Illinois with his people. Apparently on the way to Wisconsin, troops fired on and killed two braves carrying a flag of truce, and the Black Hawk War began. General Winfield Scott brought federal troops into Chicago. Their route west through DuPage County is now known as Army Trail Road. Black Hawk was driven to the Mississippi River and he offered to surrender. The troops ignored his plea for a truce and attacked at Bad Axe, Wisconsin, August 3, 1832. An American gunboat killed most of the women and children who were on the rafts in the river, and in a merciless slaughter wiped out a large part of the Indian force. Black Hawk was taken to Washington as a prisoner and finally sent back to his people in Iowa, where he died in 1838 at seventy-one.

The resulting Treaty of Chicago, concluded on September 26, 1833, forced the Indians from northern Illinois. A last powwow was held in 1835. No surveys had been made of northern Illinois and the area east of the Rock River was new to settlers and land speculators. Claims were made by plowing a furrow around as much property as the settler wished to claim on open prairies and by blazing the trees to define claim lines in groves. The most desirable claims would have both open and timber land and would include a stream or spring. When the U. S. survey had been made, the settler paid the government one dollar and twenty-five cents per acre and received a bill of sale from the U. S. land office. Claim protection or organizations were formed to discourage claim jumpers and settle boundary disputes.

The settlers to Addison Township came first from New England. In the summer of 1833, Hezekiah Dunklee left

Hillsboro, New Hampshire, and crossed the Green Mountains to Potsdam, New York, where he met Mason Smith. Traveling together, they made their way to Buffalo and boarded a boat for Detroit, where they bought a horse and wagon to cross Michigan. Reaching Chicago on September 3, 1833, they rested five days before resuming their westward journey. They crossed the Des Plaines River at the present site of Maywood, where they camped for the night with 300 Potawatomies along the river bank. The Indians were on their way to conclude the Treaty of Chicago, which would concede their land to the newcomers. The next day Dunklee and Smith followed a prairie road, later called the Elgin Road, to Salt Creek where the tent poles of General Scott's army still stood (Louis' Restaurant is there today). They crossed Salt Creek and spent the night, reaching Meacham's settlement in what is now Bloomingdale Township the next day. On September 12, 1833, they turned east from Meacham's to what is now Addison Township. They selected a homestead site east of Salt Creek on the northern edge of the large, dense woods which covered the center of the township. This woods came to be called Dunklee's Grove. The claim on Addison Township Sections 10 and 15 was made up of timberlands and prairie. A log house was built and Hezekiah Dunklee became the first freeholder of Addison Township. His family came from New Hampshire in 1834. Ebenezer Dunklee, Hezekiah's brother, settled an adjoining claim. On June 18, 1835, Julia A. Dunklee, daughter of Ebenezer and Amy Dunklee, was born, the first white child to be born in Addison Township.

Sections 10 and 15 of Addison Township are located between Salt Creek on the west and Church Road in Bensenville on the east. Dunklee's Grove has been destroyed. Patches of it survive in the Salt Creek Forest Preserve and the virgin timberland of Fischer's Woods. It was once so dense that children ventured only into the edges to pick berries. Residents of the township purchased woodlots in it to supply their homes with fuel; the oak and walnut trees furnished rafters and woodwork for houses

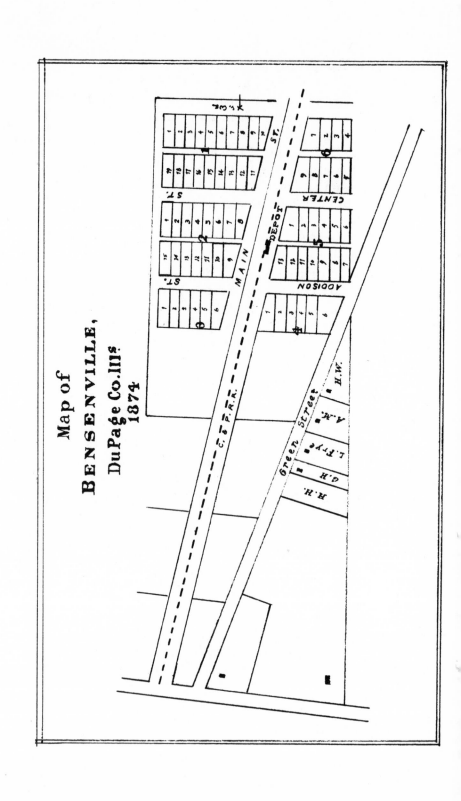

Map of
BENSENVILLE,
DuPage Co. Ills.
1874

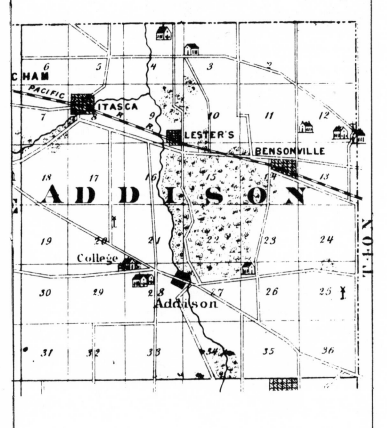

MAP OF ADDISON TOWNSHIP

No. Acres Wheat 1,436
"   "   Corn 2,371
"   "   Oats.................................... 3,845
"   "   Other Field Products 1,441
"   Horses 615
"   Cattle 2,274
"   Mules and Asses 16
"   Sheep 591
"   Hogs.. 1,082
Total Value of Domestic Animals, $90,338.

that still make up the surrounding town. Route 83 was cut into the middle of the Grove, destroying the trees that had been a source of beauty and freshness to the whole area.

Other New Englanders came in 1834. Mr. Perrin arrived that summer, dying a few weeks later, to become the first death among the new settlers. John Lester made a claim on Salt Creek in 1833 at Dunklee's Grove. In the fall of 1835, his father, Edward Lester, brought the rest of the family from New York to establish Lester's Station, the present day Wood Dale. Richard Kingston, Thomas H. Thomas, James Bean, Demerit Hoyt, E. Lamb, Thomas Williams, and D. Parsons came from New England in 1834.

Political upheavals, famine, and revolutions in Europe stimulated great waves of immigration to the United States in the middle of the nineteenth century. The surge of German immigration in the mid-1800's is largely attributable to an agricultural revolution in Germany, in which many farmers were ruined. Serious crop failures led to a major famine that extended from the Irish Sea to Russian Poland. In Germany, a new national consciousness created attempts to overthrow tyrannical leaders, and in the wake of the revolution of 1848, many Germans had to flee for their lives. These were not explorers or frontiersmen, but farmers and skilled craftsmen who preferred to establish new homes in peaceful areas similar to their homeland. They introduced soil conservation, crop rotation, and fertilization to the Midwest.

In 1833, this wave of German immigration reached the newly-opened lands of northern Illinois. Bernard Koehler is reported to be the first German settler in Addison Township. Born in Hanover, Germany, he made claim to land about one and one-half miles from the Fischer property. Frederick Graue brought his family of five sons and a daughter to a small grove in Section 34. William Henry Boske, Barney H. Franzen, Dedrick Leseman, and Frederick Kraige all came in 1834, followed by J. H. Schmidt and his son in 1835. The next year, Henry D. Fischer, J. L. Franzen, B. Kaler, D. S. Dunning, Frederick Stunckle, S. D. Pierce, C. W. Martin, and B. F. Fillmore

GERMAN SETTLERS

THE UNITED STATES OF AMERICA.

To all to whom these presents shall come, Greeting:

CERTIFICATE

Whereas John Henry Brettman, of DuPage county, Illinois, whereby it appears

has deposited in the GENERAL LAND OFFICE of the United States, a Certificate of the Register of the Land Office at Chicago

that full payment has been made by the said John Henry Brettman

according to the provisions of the act of Congress of the 24th of April, 1820, entitled "An Act making further provision for the sale of the Public Lands," for the South East

quarter of Section fourteen in Township forty north of Range three East

in the district of lands subject to sale at Chicago, Illinois, containing

one hundred and sixty acres

according to the official plat of the survey of the said Lands, returned to the General Land Office by the SURVEYOR GENERAL, which said tract has been purchased by the said

John Henry Brettman

NOW KNOW YE, That the

UNITED STATES OF AMERICA, in consideration of the Premises, and in conformity with the several acts of Congress, in such case made and provided, HAVE GIVEN AND GRANTED,

and by these presents DO GIVE AND GRANT, unto the said John Henry Brettman

and to his heirs, the said tract above described: TO HAVE AND TO HOLD the same, together with all the rights, privileges, immunities, and appurtenances of whatsoever nature,

thereunto belonging, unto the said John Henry Brettman and to his heirs and assigns forever.

IN TESTIMONY WHEREOF, I, James K. Polk,

PRESIDENT OF THE UNITED STATES OF AMERICA, have caused these letters to be made PATENT, and the SEAL of the GENERAL LAND OFFICE to be hereunto affixed.

GIVEN under my hand at the CITY OF WASHINGTON, the five day of June, in the year of our Lord one

thousand eight hundred and forty-five, and of the INDEPENDENCE OF THE UNITED STATES the sixty ninth.

By the President:

James K. Polk

By J. F. Laughlin, RECORDER OF THE GENERAL LAND OFFICE.

RECORDED, Vol. 9, PAGE 480.

came into the township. In 1837, Conrad Fischer, the father of Henry D. Fischer, arrived with his two brothers Frederick J. Fischer and August Fischer, along with William Asche.

Exact dates of arrival in DuPage County are difficult to establish and verify. Deeds were registered months or years after families laid claim and settled on the land. At the close of 1837, it is reported there were nineteen families from New England and Germany in the area. Many German families settled in the middle and southern parts of the township. These families intermarried, forming a firm matrix for community life. Having come from Hanover and Prussia in the low flat lands of northern Germany, the early settlers spoke "Plattdeutsch" or low German. High German, the language of the middle and south German highlands, was used in the churches. Plattdeutsch guilds were popular in the early years, and the Plattdeutsch Gilde Hall in Bensenville was an important social center.

FIRST HOMES

The first homes were built of handhewn logs, the beams for the roof shaped with an adz. The main room had a huge fireplace which was the source of heat and light and served for cooking. Sewing, weaving, reading, harness making, and candlemaking were all done in this room. Often the bed was here also, and the boys of the family slept in the loft above. Edwin Brettman recalls that all his brothers remembered banging their heads on the beams of his father's homestead as they scrambled into bed in the loft. The house usually included a lean-to for tools and equipment. Barns were added as the farm prospered.

BUCKHORN TAVERN

Early travelers on the stage road to Elgin and Galena could stop at the Buckhorn Tavern built in 1837 by Charles H. Holt. This building was located near Grand Avenue and York Road on what was to be the farm of Martin Luessenhop. The old tavern was Martin Luessenhop's birthplace, and when he married in 1915, the tavern was moved back from the road to make room for his new home. It was eventually torn down. It had served as a stage stop and for farmers and teamsters going to the Chicago markets. A stop at the tavern provided a meal for

Louis Brettman's homestead cabin, built about 1845

the driver, to supplement what he had brought from home, and feed for the team, if the grass on the prairie was dry. Teams came from Galena to Chicago with loads of lead from the mines. The stage road was used for all traffic between Chicago and Galena until the Chicago and Galena Union Railroad was completed in 1848.

PLANK ROADS

Plank roads were built in an effort to provide a firm surface for wheeled vehicles. Three inch boards were laid across stringers embedded in the ground at a cost of $2,000 per mile. Toll gates were set up at five mile intervals. A man on horseback paid two and one-half cents a mile, a single team and wagon cost five cents a mile, and a four horse vehicle paid seven and one-half cents a mile. By 1851 plank roads were paying 40 per cent to investors. As the planks weathered and became warped and loose, the wagons could be heard for miles around. Irving Park Road was known as the Plank Road in 1853.

FRANZEN'S MILL

In 1847, John H. Franzen established a brick factory and a flaxmill north of his farmhouse on what is now Wood Street near Barron. The grinding stones which are in Varble Park on Church Road processed flaxseed to produce linseed oil, which was in great demand. Flax became an important cash crop for the farmers around

13

Bensenville. Eventually the processing of linseed developed on a large scale in Chicago, and Franzen's discontinued their mill, but they continued in the production of flaxtow.

Originally small self-sufficient farms were established, but these yielded to the economic necessity of producing specialized crops for larger markets. Roads and later rail lines leading to markets formed the focal points for the development of villages to serve the immediate farming area. Farms ranged in size from 80 to 300 acres. The value of the land increased from one dollar and twenty-five cents in 1835 to four dollars an acre in 1848 and ten dollars an acre in 1876. A demand for wheat encouraged the farmers to send their surplus by wagon to Chicago. With the opening of wheat fields in the west, Addison Township began to raise corn for the markets. As corn production increased, the local farmers turned to general farming, stock raising, and the dairy business.

FIRST
OWNERS OF
BENSENVILLE
LAND

In 1872, the present site of Bensenville, located on Addison Township Sections 13, 14, and 23, was purchased by Dedrich Struckmann, T. R. Roddins, and Colonel Roselle M. Hough from John Lemarche. Shortly thereafter, Frederick Heuer and Henry Korthauer purchased Col. Hough's interest. Henry Korthauer had come to Addison Township in 1838 and established a farm on Section 13. Frederick Heuer's farm was on Section 10, to the north of the Plank Road. He had come in 1845. Dedrich Struckmann had come to Illinois in 1844 and was a farmer and land speculator. He had married Henry Korthauer's sister, Caroline. Frederick Heuer's daughter, Emma, was to marry Henry Korthauer's son, Herman. Col. Roselle Hough owned land in Bloomingdale Township, and the town of Roselle was named for him.

VILLAGE'S
NAME

The plat of the village that was to be Bensenville was recorded October 10, 1873. The property was subdivided into lots and a post office obtained. Old legal documents refer to Bensenville as "formerly Tioga," and local legends differ as to the origin of the name and spelling of Bensenville. One account attributes the name to an early

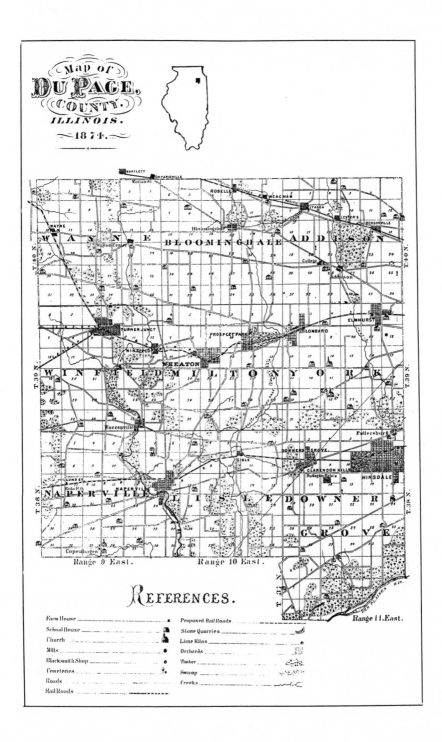

Map of DU PAGE, COUNTY. ILLINOIS. 1874.

Range 9 East.   Range 10 East.   Range 11 East.

REFERENCES.

Farm House	Proposed Rail Roads	
School House	Stone Quarries	
Church	Lime Kilns	
Mills	Orchards	
Blacksmith Shop	Timber	
Cemeteries	Swamp	
Roads	Creeks	
Rail Roads		

settler. Another story states it was the German home of a resident. *The New Combination Atlas of DuPage County 1874* spells it with an "o" and some references change the "s" to a "z". In the 1884 petition to Judge Gary for incorporation, it is stated that "the name of the proposed village will be Bensenville." Neither the petition nor the record explains why.

The original subdivision boundaries were Elmhurst (York) Road to the east, the woods along Church Road to the west, Roosevelt Street to the north, although no road existed there in 1873, and Green Street to the south. The area was considered to be well drained in the natural state. A small creek ran just north of Main Street and good water could be found at a depth of twenty feet.

EARLY RAILROAD

The railroad that served Bensenville was originally incorporated as the Atlantic and Pacific Railroad Company. The name was changed by the stockholders in 1872 to the Chicago and Pacific. The first construction was thirty-six miles of track between Halsted Street in Chicago and Elgin. There were three stations in Addison Township; Bensenville, Lester's, and Itasca. The decision to build the railroad through these villages may have been influenced by the production of dairy products by these communities. Traffic records for 1874 show that the Chicago and Pacific moved over 300,000 gallons of milk and a large volume of butter and cheese from Bensenville to Chicago. The rapid marketing system provided by the railroad encouraged dairying. The Chicago and Pacific went into receivership in May of 1876. On April 1, 1880, the Chicago, Milwaukee, and St. Paul Railway Company (the Milwaukee Road) signed a 999 year lease on the facilities, rolling stock, and property of the Chicago and Pacific. Improvements were made in the roadbed, new steel track was laid, and an artesian well sunk to the depth of 2,198 feet, 8 inches in Bensenville on railroad property between Center and Addison Streets. In 1898, the Milwaukee Road agreed to purchase outright the road, property, and franchises of the old Chicago and Pacific. This gave the Milwaukee a western route out of Chicago and provided a connection with the track southwestward from Beloit, across Illinois, to Savannah and Rock Island.

In 1884 Bensenville was the center of services to the farming community. P. T. Tiedemann had a general store in a large two-story frame building on Addison Street near the railroad. C. A. Franzen's lumberyard was across Main Street on the northwest corner. He also had a coal yard and sold feed and grain. Frank Ort had a harness making shop on Addison Street; Fred Bates was the physician and A. D. Swenson, the veterinarian. Charles Martin and Louis Schroeder had blacksmith shops. Christian Koch and Louis Marckmann each had saloons. William Struckmeyer's butter and cheese factory was on York Road in the vicinity of Laho's today. Korthauer's Hardware Store was on the northeast corner of Center and Main. Christian Baucke's house was on the corner of York and Green. The depot had two loading platforms for the milk cans the farmers brought into town by wagons. Since there were no sidewalks and the streets were not paved, they were full of dust in dry weather, and mud and ruts the rest of the time.

Drainage was to be a continuing concern of Bensenville's trustees. In August of 1884, a complaint was made to the board that water standing on Main Street between Addison and Center was creating a nuisance. The issue was tabled. Apparently September was dry, as drainage was not mentioned until the following spring. The first ordinance passed by the village established two saloon licenses, with a yearly fee of $500. Bensenville's second ordinance required that the dogs be licensed. Dogs without tags were ordered killed.

Frank Ort was appointed village marshal and empowered to arrest all vagabonds, as defined by Illinois law. A poll tax of $2 was levied on every able-bodied male inhabitant of the village to be collected by the overseers of the highways and turned over to the village treasurer. This money was paid the farmers to scrape the roads and streets. The board also paid the farmers to haul crushed rock from the quarry in Elmhurst to spread on the roads.

Concern for a school in the village had been a motivating

force for incorporation, and the board determined that it would guarantee $1,000 and half the license money for the year 1885 to the cost of a school building for District 2. One-half of the school site was to be village property and used for school purposes as long as the school building was located on it.

A sidewalk ordinance provided for the construction of wooden sidewalks five feet four inches wide. Each two inch plank was to be of good lumber, free of knots, not less than six inches or more than eight inches wide, to be nailed on a stringer with six common twenty-penny nails. These sidewalks were to be paid for by special assessment of the property owners, and if the owner refused to pay, the board ordered the sidewalk in front of his property removed.

In 1887, it was decided to compensate village officials for their work. One dollar was paid to each trustee for each board meeting attended. The clerk received fifty dollars per year, the treasurer fifteen dollars per year, the marshal fifteen dollars per year, and twenty dollars was paid to the committee on streets and alleys. The record is not clear as to whether the committee members received this money, or if it was the allocated budget for streets and alleys for the year.

To alleviate the drainage problems, a storm sewer was built in 1887. It ran south on Addison to Green Street, east on Green Street to Center, and north on Center to a pipe draining out into a slough. This sewer was paid for by special assessment. The village attempted to control railroad noise and disturbance by passing an ordinance requiring the steam engines to refrain from unnecessarily blowing their whistles, so as not to frighten the teams and to cover the chimney with a bonnet to control the smoke. The engineer was required to sound a bell or whistle when starting the train and not to exceed twelve miles an hour through the village.

Copies of all road and street plats were made by Edward Ehlers in 1888 and entered into the records in order to determine definitely the right of way for local streets. It was determined that thirty kerosene lamps were needed to

Elfring's general store on Center Street about 1910

Shop of George Frey, wagon maker, at 22 N. York Road

19

Albert Dierks' farmhouse, originally located on
Irving Park Road just east of York Road

light the village, and they would cost nine dollars per lamp.
It was necessary to hire a man to light the lamps, and the
job was let out for bids. Gustav Gutsche was hired. He
was a shoemaker, and very small. Late every afternoon he
made the rounds, pulling a cart loaded with containers of
kerosene for the lamps. He would stop at the lamp post,
climb the ladder, lift the chimney off the lamp, put in the
container of kerosene, light the wick, lower the chimney,
and descend the ladder. The lamp would burn all night, and
the next afternoon the lamplighter replaced it. The village
used kerosene street lights for twenty-two years and Gustav
Gutsche was the only lamplighter the village ever had.

On May 5, 1895, the German Evangelical Orphan and
BENSENVILLE Old Peoples Home Association of Northern Illinois laid
HOME the cornerstone for their main building just south of the
SOCIETY village limits. The brick building was on thirty acres of
farmland, and it eventually housed eighty-five orphans
and seventeen old people. A special train brought visitors,
families, and members of supporting Chicago churches to
the service and reception. The children from the Home
attended Bensenville schools and were accepted as part of
20 the community. Home festival days were exciting for

Home and shop of Gustav Gutsche, the village lamplighter and cobbler. Built about 1890, the shop was removed in 1975 to build the commuter parking lot.

Bensenville with the extra trainloads of visitors coming to town, the games, and all day picnics at the Home. The town kids often looked with envy at the life the Home kids led, and it was considered a privilege to be invited to slumber parties at the Home. The Home kids stuck together, and to attack one was to invite instant retaliation from them all. The orphan bell, which was rung at meal time was a part of the village life.

The Bensenville Record of May 3, 1895 was placed in the cornerstone of the Castle and reproductions were made in 1975 when the cornerstone opened. The paper was published in Bensenville by Henry Woodruff. News of the village board meetings, the fire department meetings, and the social events of the community were included with ads from local merchants. In the edition of May 3, 1895, Henry Ernsting was advertising a closing-out sale on his ready-made clothing; F. H. Volberding was advertising groceries, crockery, dry goods, coffee, fine oranges and choice dried fruits; Fred Elfring's ad included dress goods

Deutsches Evangel. Waisenhaus u. Altenheim, zu Altenheim, zu Bensenville, Du Page Co., Ill. - U. S. 1895.

German Evangelical Orphan and Old People's Home—1895

Dr. H. W. F. Bartells' home on York Road about 1890

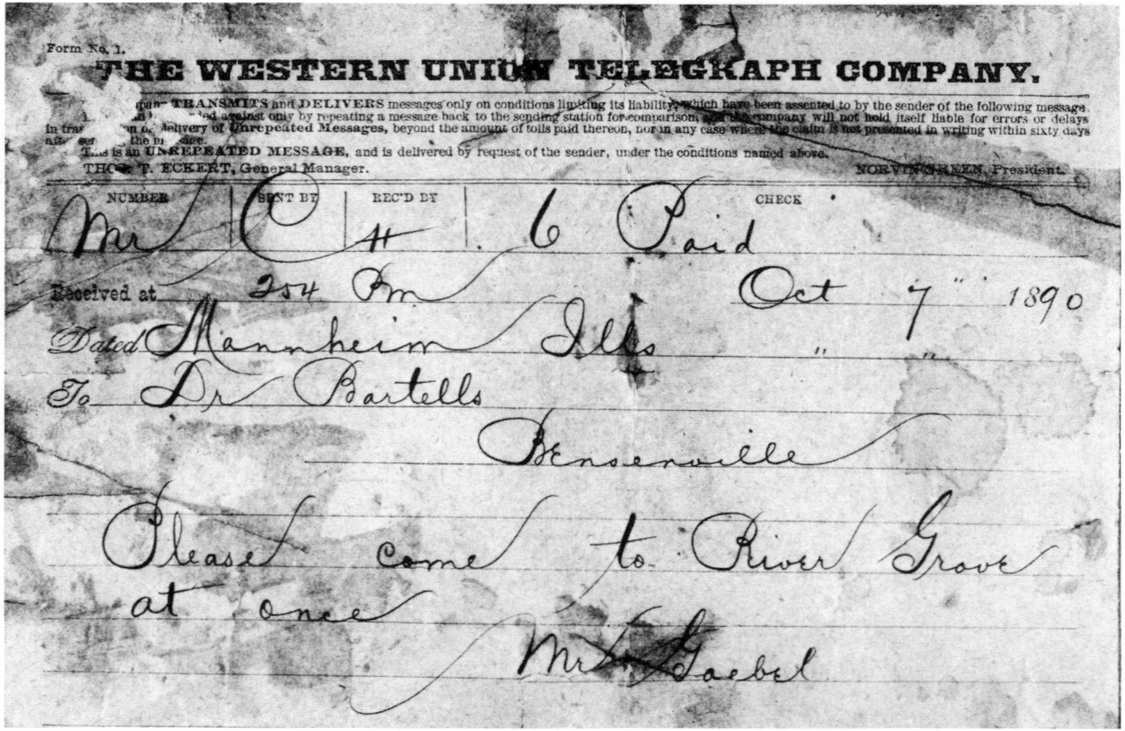

Form No. 1.

THE WESTERN UNION TELEGRAPH COMPANY.

This Company TRANSMITS and DELIVERS messages only on conditions limiting its liability, which have been assented to by the sender of the following message.
Errors can be guarded against only by repeating a message back to the sending station for comparison, and the Company will not hold itself liable for errors or delays in transmission or delivery of Unrepeated Messages, beyond the amount of tolls paid thereon, nor in any case where the claim is not presented in writing within sixty days after the message is filed with the Company for transmission.
This is an UNREPEATED MESSAGE, and is delivered by request of the sender, under the conditions named above.

THOS. T. ECKERT, General Manager.   NORVIN GREEN, President.

NUMBER	SENT BY	REC'D BY	CHECK
114	6	Paid	

Received at 2:14 p.m. Oct 7 " 1890

Dated Mannheim Ills

To Dr. Bartells
    Stonesville

Please come to River Grove
at once

Mrs. Stoebel

Telegram summoning Dr. Bartells to River Grove in 1890

Franzen-Schultz farm on Church Road, now the White Pines Club House

and trimming, provisions, boots and shoes, groceries and Dr. Ranney's Remedies. H. H. Korthauer had stoves, cutlery and carpenter's tools, steel windmills and towers, plows, cultivators, harvesters and binders; Dr. Bartell's noted calls were promptly answered day or night, and H. F. Hornbostel had a front page ad for paperhanging. Four local churches had notices of services.

SOCIAL LIFE
IN 1900

Social life in Bensenville in the 1890's and early 1900's centered around the family. On Sundays, there was visiting back and forth between the farms and the village. Immanuel Church in Churchville had an all day picnic in the summer to which the members would bring lunch to eat under the trees between the morning and afternoon services. Horseshoe Bend was a popular place for picnics. The thick pine grove between Park and Evergreen Streets had an outdoor bowling alley and dance floor which the fire department had built for their picnics. The bowling balls were kept in a box at the end of the alley, and when the grove was not being used for picnics, the Warnecke's tethered their cow on the grassy plot. A group of men formed a Mannerchor which sang at parties in the grove, often accompanied by E. A. H. Warnecke's guitar. In the winter, sleigh rides were popular. Some sleigh seats were fastened to the frame with a removable pin, to facilitate dumping an unsuspecting passenger in a snowdrift on a moonlit road. Leonard Geils remembers ice-skating on the pond east of York Road and following the frozen creek all the way to River Grove.

Homes were heated by stoves which burned coal or wood. Each family tried to own a piece of woodland which would provide some fuel. Kerosene lamps were used for light, and the upstairs bedrooms were not heated. Most families had a garden and some chickens, and maybe a pig as well as a horse and cow. Children had lots of chores to do. Fruits and vegetables were grown, picked, and canned. Water was drawn from a well, and there was no indoor plumbing.

FIRST
BANK

The Bank of Franzen Brothers was established in Bensenville in 1900. C. A. Franzen, William F. Franzen,

Church Road at Third Avenue, looking south, 1910

Mannerchor in the Pine Grove at Horseshoe Bend in 1889. Top row: ?. Louis Schmidt, Henry Korthauer, ?, P. T. Tiedemann, William Korthauer. Front: E. A. H. Warnecke, Frederick Wolkenhauer, Charles Sandhagen, ?, Louis Schroeder, ?, William Dierking, ?

E. A. H. Warnecke's home on Park, 1917

and A. W. Franzen were proprietors of the bank which was changed to the First State Bank of Bensenville on October 3, 1911. Located in a small building on Main Street, this bank is now the back of Chester Franzen's Insurance Agency. C. A. Franzen had built his large frame house to the east of the bank, and George Franzen's home was on the corner. When the change was made to a state bank, the capital stock was announced as $70,000. Apparently this attracted bank robbers who entered the bank one evening and blew the safe. The sons of C. A. Franzen, hearing the noise from their bedroom next door, loaded a shotgun and poked it out the bedroom window into the bank window below. The bank robbers were frightened off, making a clean getaway in a convenient horse and buggy standing on the street.

FIRST TELEPHONES

In 1902, the Chicago Telephone Company, forerunner of Illinois Bell, installed a phone switchboard in Korthauer's Hardware Store. George Korthauer, Sr., recalled whoever was closest to the switchboard, answered it when it rang for the operator. There were seven telephone customers in town, and they could only call each other or about sixty customers in Des Plaines. All the lines were party lines, and one time everyone was on the line at once to hear a Des Plaines band concert. Lightning set the switchboard at the store on fire during a bad storm. Mrs. Korthauer threw a bucket of water on the board, which not only put out the fire but also the telephones. It was two weeks before service was restored.

In 1897, the village board leased the Plattdeutsche Gilde Hall on the northeast corner of Center and Green for thirty dollars per year. A stove was installed, a janitor was hired, and the village furniture moved in. The Gilde Hall was used for meetings, elections, and police magistrate's court until it burned in 1903.

By 1903, it was decided to remove the wooden sidewalks and replace them with concrete walks. Three years later, the telephone company proposed to give the village twenty-five per cent discount as a courtesy for the police marshal's phone. In 1907, a board of health was appointed.

Bank of Franzen Bros. and C. A. Franzen's home on Main Street, Bensenville

William Korthauer's house, built about 1900 on Park Street

Main Street, at Center about 1910

Lincoln Ave. looking west, about 1910

J. C. Geils with his pallbearers wagon, hearse, and the mourner's carriage in front of his mortuary about 1905

Constructing the steps at Fred Mess' mortuary and furniture store on Green Street in 1912. Left to right: Fred Mess, ?, Herman H. Korthauer, George Korthauer, Sr.

Elmhurst St. (York Road) looking south, about 1910

Dr. McMurry, Henry Dierking, and H. F. Senne were responsible for advising the village board on matters pertaining to the health of the community and for deciding when a quarantine was required.

Although the streets were merely made of crush, it was necessary in 1905 to pass an automobile ordinance limiting the speed to no more than eight miles per hour. Nine lots were added to the village in 1905, when August Schwerdtfeger resubdivided block twelve of Brettman's addition. This is the block that is bordered by Green, York, Wood, and Center Streets. Mr. Schwerdtfeger had been atop a high hayrake on his farm east of town, raking his field near the railroad track, when a steam engine frightened his team. He was thrown to the ground, breaking his back. Although a tall man, his back was never straight again. He was unable to work his farm, so he moved to the village.

Sandhagen's Saloon was between Center and Addison facing the railroad. Max Fensky purchased it in 1906 and raised the building on a concrete foundation, giving the front the appearance of a loading dock. He also installed four bowling alleys. The noise from the alleys broke the peace of the saloon, so Max did not encourage much bowling. His beer was kept at fifty degrees year round, apparently an agreeable temperature which is fondly remembered. Max did not set out a free lunch, but after a couple of rounds had been ordered, he would come out with small sandwiches, usually well seasoned with very strong horseradish. Women were not welcomed in Max Fensky's, but he had the largest ice cream cones in town. Payday was celebrated by the children of the railroad employees with a nickel and a trip to Max's for a rainbow cone.

Ice, cut in the winter at Stellman's pond at County Line and Green Street, was packed in sawdust and stored in icehouses behind Max Fensky's and Thieman's, across the street. There were horse sheds there, too. Dairymen took the nine o'clock milk train into Chicago to pick up the checks for their milk. Farmers loaded vegetables, cherries,

Commuter trains have been an important part of the Milwaukee Road's presence in Bensenville since before 1900. Here a two coach train moves through the village on the way into Chicago sometime before 1920.

Fred Elfring and Fred, Jr. in the post office section of Elfring's store. Wolkenhauer's mill across Center Street can be seen through the window.

Bensenville Depot, 1915

or gooseberries onto hand-drawn platform wagons at the depot. The produce was sold at Fulton Market.

Each saloon had its own whiskey in barrels bought from the distillery and left to age. A customer brought in his own bottle or container for a quart or gallon. John Schoo remembers farmers bought whiskey this way to serve the threshers. A boy would carry a pail of fresh water and the container of whiskey to the field so the men would not have to stop work. Railroad employment increased in the 1900's. People came from other parts of the country to live in Bensenville and work on the railroad. More tracks were laid, and a stockyard pen was built on railroad property where the condominiums are at Four South Mason Street. Cattle were unloaded from the train periodically to be fed and rested. A rail switch was built into Franzen's where feed, malt, coal, and lumber were delivered. Across the street, Birk Brothers Brewery built a warehouse which was serviced by a track.

EARLY
POST
OFFICE

Bensenville's post office was in Fred Elfring's store on the east side of Center Street between Main and Roosevelt. Fred Elfring was postmaster, and he and his sons would sort the mail into cubicles. Residents would come to the store to pick up their mail. Stamps and money orders were sold, too.

Across the street was a gristmill, which had been purchased in the 1890's by Frederick Wolkenhauer whose parents had a farm northeast of town. Mr. Wolkenhauer, GRISTMILL moved his house from the farm to Center Street one winter over the frozen ground. A miller, machinist, inventor, and mystic, he was a colorful figure with flashing eyes and a long white beard. His mill ground feed for cows and horses with two stones, one flat on the floor and the other on a shaft which rotated it upon the lower stone. There was a machine shop also, and Center Street would be lined with farmers' wagons of grain to be ground, and harvesting machinery to be repaired. His front yard was full of flowers.

Lillie Wolkenhauer Lange recalls that the calaboose was behind the mill. It was a small building, with windows too

The north side of Fred Elfring's post office and store on Center Street

high in the wall for the children to see inside. Shortly before the Plattdeutsche Gilde Hall burned, the village board had ordered the village stove moved into the calaboose, in apparent concern for the comfort of the occupants. Mrs. Lange remembers that the fire hoses were occasionally hung on this cement block building to dry.

VILLAGE HALL

In 1908, plans were begun to build a village hall which would include a calaboose and space to store the fire engine. The board meetings were apparently being held on Green Street in Fred Mess' furniture store and mortuary. H. H. Korthauer, Fred Mess, and Frederick Wolkenhauer were designated a committee to draw up preliminary plans for a twenty-eight by fifty-six foot cement building with a hip roof. The village residents voted fifty-four to thirty-seven to build. Mrs. Konech's land on the southwest corner of York Road and Railroad Avenue was purchased for $850. George E. Franzen's bid of $1,416.50 for lumber and hardware, and H. C. Baucke's bid of $1,660 for mason work and materials were accepted. G. W. Ashby drew the final plans. George L. Korthauer Sr., recalled helping to make the concrete blocks, which were individually formed. The structure was completed by July 5, 1909. The Bensenville Volunteer Fire Department assembled in front of the building at ten a.m. to have their picture taken and to move the fire equipment into the new quarters.

Electricity came to Bensenville in 1910. The sale of gas for heat, light, and power was authorized in 1913. The roundhouse at the Milwaukee yards was built in 1916. It

ROUNDHOUSE

was a forty stall roundhouse, employing three hundred people. The engine turntable was in the center with the stalls around the outer circumference for the maintenance of the steam engines. It was the home shop for the Milwaukee Road. It brought many new people into town, provided jobs and business which boosted the town's economy, and increased the demand for housing and services. Many new families felt strange and unwelcome in the settled German town. Railroad engineers began to build houses in the village, and Bensenville became more of a railroad town than a German farming community.

On July 5, 1909, the fire engine, a hand pumper was moved to the new village hall at 10:00 A.M., and this picture taken. Members of the fire department are left to right, top row: William Franzen, Village President, Gustav Gutsche, J. C. Geils, Victor Beck, W. F. Dunteman, Ernst Schultz, Edwin Freie, Fred H. Volberding, Henry Thieman. Bottom row: left to right, H. L. Geils, Fred Mess, J. T. Tiedemann, Fred Koelker, Louis Grobe, Henry Marshall, George E. Franzen, Carl Kirchoff, F. H. Wolkenhauer, H. H. Korthauer, Ernst Boldebuck, Louis Brettman, Ed Freie.

Aerial view of the Milwaukee roundhouse on Green Street

Horseshoe Bend, 1919, with the pine grove in the center. The smoke stacks from the roundhouse can be seen in the background.

The roundhouse and the freight yard changed the direction of Bensenville's economic and physical growth. The smoke and dirt killed the pines at Horseshoe Bend between Park and Evergreen, which had originally been planned as a parkway for a double boulevard. Housewives struggled with soot and smoke in their laundry and curtains. Homes were built to the west of the area.

World War I increased the railroad traffic, and the yards were busier. Although anti-German feeling swept the country, Bensenville had young men from German and non-German families enlist in the army and navy. In 1917, Carl Kirchoff represented the village board at a county meeting to plan a send-off for DuPage recruits leaving for various camps. At the end of the war, the returning soldiers became anxious for the well-being of the people at home, as reports of the flu epidemic made them fearful their families were being wiped out.

Prohibition in 1920 must have been difficult in a town with five saloons. Near beer was legally sold, and it is reported families could make home brew without interference.

MUNICIPAL WATERWORKS

By 1922, the village board was planning a referendum to authorize the issuing of bonds to develop a municipal waterworks system which would include a well, pumping station, pumping machinery, water main system, and above ground tank. This system was to cost $20,000, and it carried at a special election by a one hundred forty-seven to fifty-seven vote. The water main system was financed by a special assessment and applicants for tapping into the water system paid twenty-four dollars. The water tank on York Road was constructed by the Chicago Bridge and Iron Works for $8,185 on a foundation built by Ehlers

DuPage County World War I Army recruits in camp at Waco, Texas
Standing: Owen Kindy, Frank Koebbeman, Pat Murphy
Seated: Otto Herr, Herman Miller, George Korthauer, Richard Andorf

Pumphouse

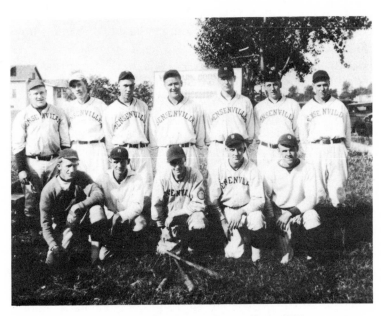

Bensenville Baseball Team—Early '30's

Brothers in 1924. It is a 75,000 gallon steel tank on a one hundred foot tower and is still used by the village as a supplementary elevated water supply for Bensenville's water system.

In 1927, a new house numbering system was begun, sanitary sewers and the disposal plant installed, and the street and pavement project costing $386,141.11 came to a vote. Water meters were read by a meter reader who gave the householder his water bill immediately. This was to be taken to the village hall to be paid. More land was annexed to the village as subdivisions. Barney Franzen's farm was developed into Mohawk Golf Club. The First State Bank of Bensenville was built on the corner of Main and Addison. The village began to feel the need for **NEED OF INDUSTRY** industrial areas, and land was zoned to attract industries from Chicago. This industrial area was east of York Road and north of the railroad tracks. The stock market crash of 1929 brought a slowdown in construction and expansion. The proposed industrial development did not materialize.

Baseball was a big attraction in the '20's. Young boys played ball in empty lots and longed to get on the local Cardinal team. Sunday afternoons were taken up with baseball games. The Bensenville Businessmen's Association purchased the suits and equipment. An Oldtimer's Baseball League was established.

By the mid-1930's, many greenhouses had been built in DuPage County, and they had become a vital part of Bensenville's economy. The Breiter family built greenhouses on both sides of Church Road; W. F. Dunteman's greenhouses were on the north side of Green Street, east of the school. The Leider family bought out Mr. Dunteman in 1941. Edward Garry's nursery and greenhouses were built on Irving Park Road in 1941.

Ed Sprandel built a modern store and apartments on the corner of Center and Green and moved his business into it. On the next corner at Addison, Joe Jankers built a business building and apartments, with an ice cream parlor in the corner store. Outdoor movies were replaced by a movie theater on Center Street, and four new stores

Center Street 1927. The theater and four stores had just been built. The street was not paved.

were added to provide the village with a business block. The post office moved into one, with George Warnecke as postmaster. Center Street was paved late in 1927. There was a dance pavilion behind Kebbies' on Addison with wide windows that opened up and out for summer dances. Franzen's Hall, over the lumberyard's office building, held dances in cold weather and was the meeting place for community organizations. Card parties and family get-togethers filled people's leisure time.

The responsibilities of the village had grown, and as services to the community grew, the number of village employees should have grown. The depression caused a cutback in funds the village had available for services, and only such improvements as were absolutely necessary, such as laying additional water mains or paving streets in cooperation with the federal government's W.P.A. program, were undertaken.

Some families survived the depression without grave problems. But there were children who went to school hungry and families who lost homes and property. The Milwaukee Women's Club, which was begun as a benevolent social organization, brought groceries and paid bills for

DEPRESSION YEARS

Milwaukee Women's Club Chapter 3, Bensenville, 1929. The club house was constructed of two box cars placed on railroad property between York Road and Center Street. It housed a small library, the first in Bensenville. From left to right: Mrs. Elizabeth DiVall, Mrs. Elliot, Mrs. Stella Sampson, Mrs. Olga Bodenberger, Mrs. O'Keefe, Mrs. Sutherland, Mrs. Dora Tonning, Mrs. Louise Suter, Mrs. Divinney, ?, Mrs. Alice Harney, Mrs. Mary Holquist, Mrs. Betty Lackner, Mrs. Olive Hugdahl, Mrs. Melvin, Mrs. Schnell, Mrs. Toland, Mrs. Rands. Standing: Mrs. Bartholmey, Mrs. Emma Capoot, Mrs. Ethel Bracke, Mrs. Byers, Mrs. Lee

needy families. They helped railroad families who had been put on short time or laid off from the railroad. Their clubhouse on railroad property housed the first library in town. Chester Franzen opened the currency exchange and insurance office on Main Street, serving as bill collector, legal advisor, and father confessor. Some families bought inexpensive lots near town and built small houses or garages to live in until times improved.

Bensenville made the newspapers as the hideout for two separate kidnapping cases. William Hamm, Jr., from St. Paul, Minnesota, was held in a house on York Road, from which he was taken to Minnesota and freed on payment of ransom. Edward G. Bremer, also from St. Paul, was held for about twenty days in a barn on Green Street east of York Road. He, too, was released by the Karpis-Barker gang that was responsible for both kidnappings.

The school system did have to delay payment of teacher salaries in 1931, as they had no funds. The teachers living with families in town were granted extensions on their rent. Before the end of the year, the money became available, and the teachers were paid. Farming became important again as a source of food, but more people were employed in industry and business than agriculture.

The Bensenville Community Credit Union was established in 1932 by Francis Suter. People needed loans. He got fifty signatures from Bensenville residents in order to get the charter. The first credit union office was in his home, and later in his insurance office on Green Street. This credit union is one of the few community credit unions ever established.

Mrs. Ralph Howell, Miss Florence Rockwood, and Mrs. Fred Rockwood opened a restaurant in 1932 in a log cabin on the Grove property with one cook, one dishwasher, and five girls from Bensenville as waitresses. The building was built of logs cut on the property. As the business grew, more logs would be cut and rooms added on. Originally, Plentywood had no sidewalks, and people had to walk in from Grove Street when the ground was wet.

In 1937, Stresen-Reuter, a manufacturer of paints,

PLENTYWOOD FARM

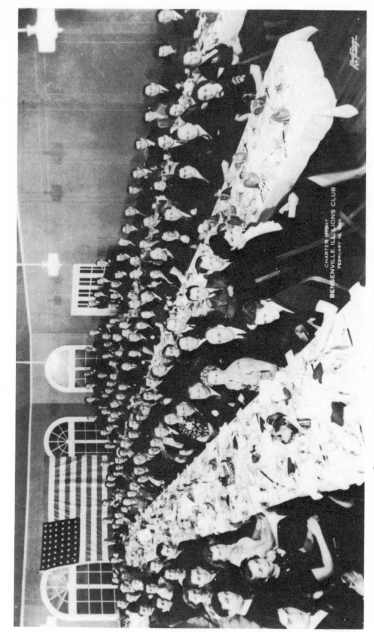

Charter night, Bensenville Lions Club, February 14, 1939

Plentywood Farm, about 1925. Ernst Mechlinberg, the nursery man is standing with George Grove approximately where the restaurant is located today.

varnishes, and chemicals moved into the factory building on Main Street that had processed milk. This brought some additional employment to town. It also began the controversy that was to rage a long time as to the type of community Bensenville was to be; a residential community with a few small businesses, or a town with industries to provide employment and funds.

During the depression, people would charge things at the local stores and hope the money would be forthcoming at the end of the month. It is said that the local merchants attempted to carry individual items in their stock so that the trade was distributed through the town. Eggs sold at one store, bread at another. People slowed down their activities that cost money and hoped the depression would soon be over. Dorothy Dean bought some pencils her brother could not use and sold them to her classes for five cents apiece. The money went into a fund the classes then used for emergencies among its members. Teachers were careful to see that students used both sides of a piece of paper before it was discarded. Teachers took turns cooking lunch at school, as there was no lunchroom and it cost less to do their own cooking. There were not many restaurants in town. Some teachers got their lunches from the family with whom they boarded. Mrs. Peck provided her boarding teachers with four big sandwiches and an apple for twenty-five cents.

The yearly tax appropriation for 1939 to operate the village was $38,470. The trustees were paid three dollars a meeting, and the village president received $360 per year. Mable Gjectsen was paid four dollars for making the pattern for village traffic signs.

The population of Bensenville in 1940 was 1,875. There were 195 more people in town than in 1930. There would be an increase of 100 per cent in the next ten years. It would never be a quiet, underdeveloped village again.

BEGINNINGS
OF
O'HARE FIELD

The Douglas aircraft plant at the present O'Hare Field was built by the U. S. government during World War II to produce Douglas C-54 "Skymaster" cargo planes. The location was selected because it was neither industrially

Center Street, 1937

nor residentially developed, and it was close to a relatively untapped labor supply. The land costs were considered reasonable, and there was an established commuter service nearby. By July, 1942, bulldozers were clearing the farms of houses and barns, and by August of 1943, the plant was completed. Six hundred fifty-five large cargo planes were delivered to the armed forces from August, 1943 to October, 1945. Bensenville residents found jobs at Douglas, and people coming into the area to work at Douglas looked for housing in Bensenville. Some homes were built during the war on vacant lots in the developed part of town. War economy restrictions limited the houses to 900 square feet of living area. The buyer had to be employed in the war effort.

The draft board, ration board, stamps for meat, butter, sugar, coffee, and gasoline all became a part of village life.

Wesley Poor, as a boy, stood in line to spend the family meat stamps at the grocery on Center Street and was rewarded with a nickel coke at the pharmacy. Water bills were collected at the Suter's office, where birth and death records were also kept. High school students were recruited as civil defense runners, and boys went to war immediately upon graduation from high school. Tables were set up on the gym stage at BCHS for the Red Cross blood drive. The village established plots for victory gardens on Grove Street, between Barron and Church Road.

Francis Suter was village clerk and coordinator of Civil Defense. Each block in the village had an air raid warden to help enforce the blackout rules. It was felt that Bensenville might be vulnerable to an air strike because of the proximity of the Douglas plant and the railroad yards. Periodic drills were held to train the residents in case of an emergency, but the novelty of a blackout drill wore off. People became lax and did not always turn out the lights or close the shades. Mrs. Suter recalls the mayor, William Peck and Armin Korthauer, the Public Works Superintendent got together and decided Bensenville would have a complete blackout or know the reason why. Armin Korthauer got some giant firecrackers or bombs from the

Bensenville Yards in the late 1940's. To the left a steam locomotive moves railroad cars, making up an outbound freight from a classification track. To the right is a small diesel switching locomotive.

Franklin Park fireworks factory. Francis Suter issued the blackout order from the command post in the basement of the village hall. A few minutes after the sirens blew, the bombs went off. The town went so dark, it could not be seen with a candle. Reporters called from Chicago to ask what was going on in Bensenville.

The village truck was made available to pick up tin cans for the war effort. The Lions Club erected a roll of honor for servicemen, on York Road, which was lighted at night with the lights from the pump house. Lena Bachelor was elected village clerk, but after serving three months, she moved away, when her army chaplain husband was transferred. Louise Suter took over, working out of the Suter office on Green Street. William Redmond became village attorney. In 1975, William Redmond was elected Speaker of the Illinois House of Representatives.

Bensenville still had drainage problems in the '40's. Many of the roads in Bensenville were graveled. Armin Korthauer remembers that Green Street near County Line had ruts a couple of feet deep. The Austin-Western grader would get stuck as they tried to scrape the road. The only equipment the village had was the grader, an old second-hand dump truck, and a pickup.

THE VFW

During the war, Bensenville suffered a number of casualties. The Paddock newspaper covered every death with a complete family background and history of the serviceman. During the war, the VFW bought the Social Hall on York Road from Joe Jankers. Francis Suter, Robert Smith, and James Means convinced George Grobe to sell the bar. They issued loyalty bonds to raise money. When the returning soldiers arrived home, the membership increased and the VFW became one of the most active organizations in town. In 1946, they donated $21,000 to a lighting fund for the high school. Ray Soden, a member of Bensenville's VFW Post #2149, was elected national commander-in-chief in 1973-74.

Chicago purchased Douglas Field from the army in 1946, and announced they would purchase 1,900 farms to expand the airport. The following year, the village board was informed by the airport developer that O'Hare would expand to 6,300 acres, and that the Chicago and Northwestern tracks would be relocated through the village. A petition was circulated which stated that Chicago had no right to condemn property in DuPage County. William Redmond, who was also a member of the State Legislature, was quoted as saying he would go to the General Assembly for help if Chicago would not change its plans. A change in the number of planned runways at O'Hare eliminated the need to divert a railroad through Bensenville.

In June of 1945, Otto Kresnicka sold his pharmacy on Center Street to John Duerkop, who was a captain in the army. The first week he owned the pharmacy, Capt. Duerkop was still in uniform. He had not yet hired anyone to help in the store and he could not get away long enough to purchase civilian clothes. The A&P had stores built onto the block of Center Street in 1928, and about 1941, four new stores had been added to the south. They included Elynor Reid's Dress Shop, Walker's Jewelry Store, a hardware store owned by Fred Koebbeman and Walter Kehoe, and the meat market at the end owned by the Schoo's and Louis Oehlerking. Chester Franzen remodeled the front of his insurance agency on Main Street extending the improvement down the block to the alley. Barbara Linden reported to the village board that in order to improve parks in the village, a park board should be set up. The Mohawk subdivision was annexed to the village, and homes were begun in White Pines. On October 2, 1947, notice was given of a meeting of the village board and the firemen's committee to discuss the building of a new fire station.

After World War II, people were eager to build peaceful communities. Martin Romme remembers that the servicemen returned to settle down and work, sometimes at two jobs, to establish a home and family life. Churches, scouting, the VFW, Lions, PTA's, and athletic programs boomed. The do-it-yourself attitude extended from home repairs to painting classrooms. Home owner associations formed to develop friendship among newcomers and

Looking north on Church Road, near Irving Park, in 1960, as the caterpiller grades the road.

Lowering well No. 3, at the corner of Church Road and Main Street, April 15, 1960

promote the interests of new subdivisions. School problems attracted citizen advisory groups who actively worked to pass school referendums.

The business community expanded with the population. In 1946, the Bensenville Chamber of Commerce was organized, working immediately on projects to benefit the village. Stop signs, parking areas, mosquito and smoke abatement, bus service, youth programs, the welcome wagon, and a new post office were public service matters the Chamber promoted. Freida Milstreich, who was the Chamber secretary for 15 years, recalls that it was a busy and happy time as Bensenville grew.

The sale of farmland at O'Hare radically changed the character of the area. Truck farms disappeared and industrial areas took their place. The village government outgrew the village hall and the town outgrew the sanitation system. A developer bought the Franzen lumberyard and built Park and Shop at Addison and Main. Fred Mess had operated a yard there for some years, but the original two-ton safe had remained in the building. John Duerkop bought the safe, intending to use it in his pharmacy. It was too heavy to move into his new store, so he gave it to the fire department, who did manage to put it in their new firehall. The week after Duerkop's Pharmacy moved to Park and Shop, George Wilkinson established his pharmacy on Center Street and Bensenville had two drugstores for the first time.

Noise pollution had not yet become a matter of concern in Bensenville, but Police Chief Harry Kolze ticketed the engineer of a steam locomotive for blocking the crossing at York Road and filling the air with black smoke. The cooker at Stresen-Reuter produced a colored smoke which hung over the center of town and was very odoriferous. Periodic checks by village inspectors produced many assertions of controls to be added, and finally filters were installed which prevented the fumes from escaping into the air.

The sewer and water systems were enlarged. Ninety homes were built south of the Bensenville Home and east of York Road. The Suter subdivision was developed on Wood Street near St. Alexis Church. Joe Krass was the builder, and Francis Suter was the "land man". Lowell Capoot, who had talked Herb Dierking into running for village clerk, moved to Texas, and Gust Van Mol was elected president of the village board. As the farming community diminished, a lumberyard replaced the feed company in town.

In the mid-1950's, an organization began to take options on property north of Irving Park and the Mohawk subdivision between York Road and Route 83. After a number of options had been taken, the village annexed the land and put in sewers and water. This was to be the beginning and largest part of Bensenville's industrial area.

TREE TOWNS
WATER
COMMISSION

Neighboring towns were becoming concerned that their water tables were dropping. The Tree Towns Water Commission proposed to build a pipeline and invited all other towns along the route to take part. Bensenville's village board decided to sign a contract with the Tree Towns Commission to participate as Bensenville's water table dropped from forty to sixty feet per year. The states bordering Lake Michigan sued the Tree Towns Commission to prevent their use of Lake Michigan water. Although the final court decision ruled against the Tree Towns, the issue was reactivated in 1975, when the Illinois Division of Waterways of the Department of Transportation elected to reopen public hearings.

Aircraft lights were put on the top of the elevated water tower on York Road in 1956. The same year, the village paid $15,000 of a total cost of $73,000 for four crossing gates on the railroad tracks. It was reported that Pine Lane was not passable, and Mr. Kaufman was instructed to go up and down the street and collect whatever money he could from the residents for crushed stone, and the village would pay the balance to cover the road. Library Day was established, and citizens asked to donate books to start the local library collection. A group of citizens organized a not-for-profit committee to build a swimming pool. Chips Ortega was the chairman. A

Recreation and Park Commission was created in May of 1956 with William Redmond as chairman, Matthew Sirvek and Mrs. Jerome Carrol as commissioners.

In 1956, a referendum was held to establish a Fire and Police Commission. It passed on May 15, and sixty days from that date went into effect. The policemen and any new firemen hired by the village were under U. S. Civil Service. A commission was appointed which would handle complaints, interviews, and testing for members of the police and fire departments.

In 1959, Bensenville purchased eight acres on the corner of Church Road and Main Street from Alfred and Freida Kolze for $46,000. This farm had a house and small farm buildings on it. The house was leased to the Library and the village paid for the renovating. This farm was to eventually be the site of the village hall, the water tower, the underground reservoir and the Public Safety Building.

NEW VILLAGE HALL

Late in 1959, the Chicago, Milwaukee, and Pacific Railroad informed the village board that they were interested in buying the Mohawk Golf Club to develop an industrial area. The residents of the subdivision protested. In January of 1960, the village annexed Mohawk Golf Club. Fred Steging recalls arrangements were worked out in 1966 with the Milwaukee Land Company and Clearing Industrial District to develop the property as an industrial area for Bensenville.

Demands on the village services grew constantly. The Luessenhop farm at Grand and York became the Brentwood subdivision, and a new shopping area was developed. The sewer treatment plant was enlarged, and a new well was installed in the new industrial area.

During the 1960 presidential campaign, John F. Kennedy flew into O'Hare to appear in the western suburbs. He spoke at Elmhurst's York High School, traveling through Bensenville on his return to the motel. Crowds waited until after 11 p.m. in front of the VFW for his brief appearance in Bensenville.

Although the population of Bensenville had grown, vestiges of a small village community remained. Village

Chips Ortega, Scott Kinneman, Fred Koebbeman, and Walter Kehoe in the Hardware Store on Center Street in 1950

Paving Mason Street from Wood to Memorial in 1960

Mohawk Country Club House

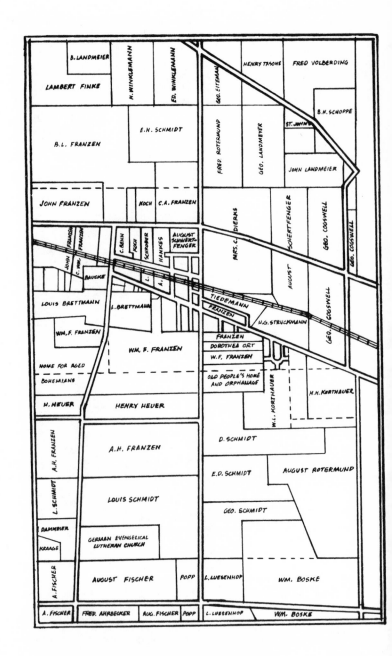

Bensenville Area Landowners
Approximately 1900

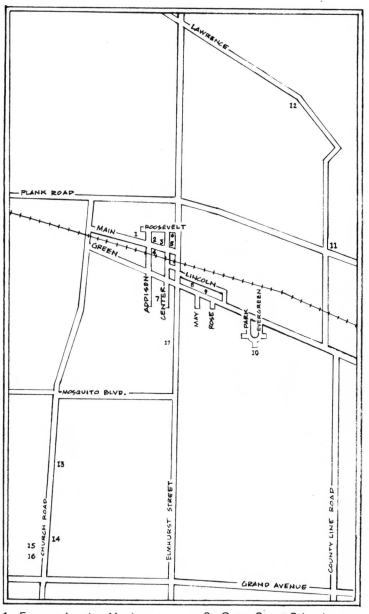

**Bensenville
Area**

**Approximately
1900**

1. Franzen Lumber Yard
2. Bank of Franzen Brothers
3. Volberding's Store
4. Tiedemann's Store
5. Korthauer's Hardware Store
6. Elfring's Store
7. Peace Church
8. E. U. B. Church

9. Green Street School
10. Horseshoe Bend
11. Cogswell's Corner
12. St. John's Church & Cemetery
13. Franzen-Schultz Farm
14. Zion Church
15. Churchville School
16. Immanuel Church
17. J. C. Geils' Mortuary

presidents were often called by residents wanting to discuss their problems with someone who might help. President Richie Thomas received a call from one irate citizen demanding to know what Mr. Thomas intended to do about the squirrels who were eating the caller's pears.

New residents moved out to Bensenville from the city, attracted by the pleasant town and availability of transportation to their jobs. Industry brought in people from other parts of the country, and many people lived in Bensenville but were not a part of the community. As land for individual homes became scarce, apartment buildings were built to provide homes close to the new local industry.

Noise from the increased jet traffic at O'Hare began to be a problem to Bensenville residents in the 1960's. Although the value of residential real estate remained comparable to other suburbs, and the price of vacant land continued to rise, residents found the roar from jet engines deafening and nerve-racking. John Varble, as president of the village's board of trustees, assumed leadership in N.O.I.S.E., the National Organization to Insure a Sound-Controlled Environment, to work to alleviate the elevated levels of jet sound over the towns around airports. New flight patterns, particularly at night, were adopted to avoid the noise.

N.O.I.S.E.

The village board appointed Harold Koehler as administrative assistant of the village in 1966. The original concept of government by community members on a voluntary part-time basis could not meet the requirements of operating a municipality in the 1960's. Representative government was still in effect, but the professional administrators, responsible to an elected board, were necessary to make the system work. Various functions of village government became departments, run by professionals who reported to the village administrator.

Paul Schriever was appointed village administrator in 1974. As a member of all the village committees, he oversees the total operation of the village, and is the liaison between the departments and the board of trustees. No longer do the local board members haul crush for the

Current aerial view of the Bensenville Yard, one of the largest and most modern automatic freight classification yards in the United States. View is to the east with downtown Chicago visible in the distance.

Senior Citizens on the Village float in 1975 Fourth of July Parade. Mrs. and Mr. Walter Olhaber, Mrs. Celia Webb, Vining Jacobs, Mrs. Lillian Mueller

Mohawk subdivision, aerial view, 1959

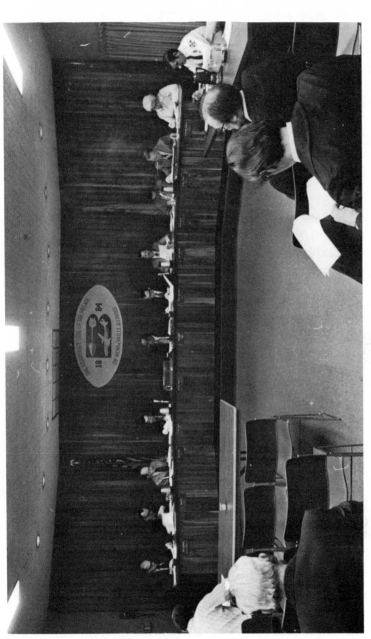

1976 Bensenville Village Board. Left to right: Paul Schriever, Village Administrator, Trustee John Kral, Trustee Berni Zoden, Trustee Sid Ceaser, Village President James DiOrio, Village Clerk Fred Valentino, Trustee Louis Spillone, Trustee William Bourke, Trustee Richard Weber, Secretary Kay Murphy

roads with their own teams of horses or draft their own legal documents. Village government has evolved into a council-manager system, and professional administrators are found in every tax supported institution in Bensenville. Local governments began to feel financial pressures which could be relieved by federal funding of village programs. Traditional political assumptions of local control, voluntary effort, and self-regulation seemed threatened by the interjection of federal money. The growth of the village demanded larger services, and gradually the concept of asking for federal grants became accepted. The new fire station and the aerial truck, the commuter parking lot, civil defense, senior citizens, the youth commission, dial-a-bus, have all received federal funds. The $7.6 million tertiary treatment plant being built has received $5.8 million in federal funds; the rest will be raised by a bond issue.

MEMBERS OF THE VILLAGE OF BENSENVILLE BOARD OF TRUSTEES

Louis Brettman	1890-1891, 1899-1905
William F. Franzen	1890-1897. President 1898-1912, 1919-1921
August Asche	President 1891-1892. Trustee 1894-1899
Herman L. Geils	1891-1899
Christian Koch	1892-1894
Alex Schmidt	1892-1894
Charles Wellner	Clerk 1892-1895. Trustee 1898-1902
H. W. F. Bartels	1894-1896
Fred Elfring	1894-1899. President 1913-1914, 1921-1922
Charles H. McNay	Clerk 1896-1898
E. A. H. Warnecke	1897-1907
Henry Sandhagen	Clerk 1898-1904
Fred J. Mess	1899-1911
H. F. Senne	1899-1900, 1908-1912 President 1914-1919
A. D. Rotermund	1902-1904
John C. Geils	1902-1908, 1909-1911
Fred Koelker	1904-1910
Edward B. Freie	Clerk 1904-1911
E. M. Boldebuck	1905-1909, 1913-1917, 1919-1921, 1924-1934
Frederick Wolkenhauer	1907-1909
Christ H. Frase	1909-1912
E. A. Schultz	1910-1918
Meyer Meyer	1911-1914
William H. Koebbeman	Clerk 1911-1920
Ernst Seilkop	1912-1913
George Runge	1913-1921, 1923-1925. President 1929-1935, 1936-1937
Henry Holt	1913-1917
W. F. Dunteman	1913-1920
Fred C. Warnecke	1914-1922, 1923-1927
Fred Landmeier	1917-1919
A. H. Pierron	1918-1920
William Ernsting	1917-1919 Treasurer 1921-1923, 1925-1926
I. W. Riggins	1919-1921
G. F. Brentner	1920-1922
Max Fensky	1920-1922, 1927-1931

73

VILLAGE OF BENSENVILLE PRESIDENTS

George Cogswell	1884-1885
B. L. Franzen	1885-1886
William Struckmeyer	1886-1887
George Cogswell	1887-1889
P. T. Tiedemann	1889-1891
August Asche	1891-1892
Herman H. Korthauer	1892-1897
Charles E. Martin	1897-1898
William F. Franzen	1898-1913
Fred Elfring	1913-1914
Henry F. Senne	1914-1919
William F. Franzen	1919-1921
Fred Elfring	1921-1922
Herman H. Korthauer	1922-1929
George Runge	1929-1935
Wade Williams	1935
Leonard Geils	1935-1936
George Runge	1936-1937
William B. Peck	1937-1949
Lowell Capoot	1949-1954
Gust Van Mol	1954-1961
Richard D. Thomas	1961-1965
Fred Steging	1965-1969
John Varble	1969-1974
James DiOrio	1974-

THE SCHOOLS

School District 2 was formed from portions of Districts 3 and 8 in April, 1885, at a public meeting in Bensenville a year after the village was incorporated. The record of the meeting does not indicate the place or the number of citizens attending, but George Cogswell, C. A. Franzen, and Herman H. Korthauer were elected school directors. They were to receive bids for a proper school site, have plans and specifications made for a school building, and get estimates for the total cost. George Cogswell was elected the first president of District 2, and Herman H. Korthauer the first clerk. On May 26, 1885, the second meeting was held, "whereupon the balloting of the school site commenced. The result was that the directors bought lots 6, 7, 8, 9 and 22, 23, 24 and 25 of Block 4 of Brettman's addition to Bensenville, at a cost of $775." This property was to be held jointly with the village as long as a school building be located thereon.

Plans drawn by Herman H. Korthauer for a two-story frame building were accepted. There was to be a primary room on the first floor and a room for the higher grades upstairs. In October, the directors were authorized to issue bonds in the amount of $2,000 to pay for the building. Christian Baucke's bid for $527 for masonry and Greimen's bid of $793 for carpentry work were accepted. The

FIRST GREEN STREET SCHOOL

building was to be completed in October, 1886, at a total cost of $3,095.

Early board meeting minutes indicate that the directors met formally once a year. In April, 1886, the directors decided the upper room be furnished, the school be graded, that two teachers be hired, and that the principal be installed for ten months. Herman H. Korthauer presented trees to be planted around the new building. School must have begun in 1886, as the Churchville School records note a drop in enrollment at Churchville School from eighty in 1885 to thirty in 1886, due to the Bensenville school children attending another school. The first record in District 2's minutes of teacher contracts is in 1900, when T. A. Gallagher was hired to act as principal and teacher at a salary of sixty-five dollars per month. Miss Kate Hauck was hired to teach the lower grades at forty-five dollars per month. The school levy for this year was $1,200.

By 1900, almost one hundred pupils attended Green Street School, so it became necessary to consider hiring a third teacher. It was decided to divide the first floor into two rooms, and hire a teacher capable of teaching both German and English. The board decided to allow a week off at Christmas. In 1906, it was decided to use the school for German classes in the summer. In 1909, the wooden sidewalks were taken up and cinder walks put in. Bids were taken that year for cement walks. The annual school directors' meeting at the schoolhouse was concerned with letting bids for coal to heat the school, determine the tax levy, decide on teacher contracts, and approve bills.

In 1914, Green Street School had ninety-seven pupils and three eighth grade graduates. Two years later, the frame building was considered overcrowded and was condemned by the public authorities. Notices were posted in the three most public places in the school district, the post office, First State Bank, and Teidemann's Store, for a referendum for approval of the erection of a new Green Street School, with a bond issue in the amount of $27,000. The bid was let to Henry E. Marckhoff and Son for $21,814 plus additional costs of $2,300 for heating and ventilating. The

George Noller and George Boldebuck stretched out on the grass in front of the downstairs or primary group at the original Green Street School

original building was sold at public auction and moved to the west, to 15 West Green Street, where it stood until the present Green Street Store was built.

The new brick Green Street School was opened in 1917, with four teachers and the principal, Leo Fredericks. The curriculum included reading, writing, arithmetic, spelling, history, and geography. There were four rooms on the first floor, two grades to an elementary schoolroom. The total enrollment was 105 pupils. The original light fixtures were single cord lights, six to a room, which hung down from the ceiling. Each room was equipped with an oak clock, spring wound, with a swinging pendulum. On the second floor was an auditorium in which the first Bensenville high school was begun in 1917. The principal taught the high school subjects. There were sixteen students in the ninth and tenth grades. A Victrola, piano, and sheet music were purchased. Books were purchased by the parents of the pupils at Teidemann's Store.

Mrs. Erna Ehlers Hackmeister, who taught at both the old and new Green Street Schools, recalls the children were well behaved, although she had two grades in one room. Teachers were responsible for developing the work covered during the year within the curriculum set forth by the school directors. Mrs. Edna McAlpine Peterson, who came to teach in Bensenville in 1919, remembers how friendly the town was to teachers. A young student cautioned her the first week to be sure to speak to everyone she met on the street, as the citizens wanted to be friendly.

After serving as principal and teacher for seven years, Leo Frederick resigned in 1918 to enter military service. George Sykes replaced him as principal. In June, 1921, Fred C. Fenton, a native of Nebraska and a graduate of Aurora College, was hired as principal. By this time, the total population of District 2 exceeded 1,000, and it became necessary under the law to reorganize the district with a seven-man board. At the school election of April, 1922, Jessie O. Capoot was elected the first president of the school district, Harry Geils, George Runge, Carleton

Mr. Hench and the Bensenville Green Street School students. 1st row: ?, ?, ?, ?, Laura Ernsting, Herbie Geils, Richard Landmeier, Irvin Franzen. 2nd row: Henry Ahlborn, Lily Freie, Hattie Koebbeman, Hattie Franzen, Luch Schmidt, Julius Frey. 3rd row: ?, Otto Hueber, ?, Matt Randecker, ?, ?, Fred Elfring. 4th row: George Warnecke, Alvin Kuehn, Rose Volberding, Rose Meyer, ?, Clara Meyer, Leonard Geils, George Korthauer.

Green Street school, built in 1917

Brown, George F. Breutner, W. A. Ernsting, and J. C. Geils were elected to the board. Mr. Fenton's title was changed to superintendent, but he continued to teach at the high school level. Three years of high school was offered.

It became necessary to rent the main floor of the village hall and assign the seventh grade classes to it. Seven elementary teachers taught the first seven grades. A portable classroom building was erected to the east of the school in 1924 for the fifth and sixth grades. The eighth grade was taught on the second floor at Green Street in the auditorium with the high school classes. The basement provided space for washrooms, storage, indoor play areas, and the boiler room.

CLASSES IN THE VILLAGE HALL

Wesley A. Johnson, in his discussion of Bensenville school development, points out that the entire operation, grade school and high school, was strictly a District 2 program, essentially a local village school.

Early in 1925, the Community High School District 100 was organized in the villages of Bensenville and Wood Dale. It even extended into the village of Addison. It was originally bounded on the north and east by Cook County, and extended south to the intersection of York Road and Lake Street. Legal objections raised by some residents required over a year of litigation before approval of the new district was achieved. The high school district was validated by action of the State Supreme Court in 1926. Five community high school board members were elected: William Dunteman, president, Benjamin H. Schmidt, secretary, Walter Olhaber, Carleton L. Brown, and Harry Geils, members.

HIGH SCHOOL DISTRICT FORMED

Wesley A. Johnson was hired as the first science teacher, athletic coach, and assistant principal in 1926. He recalls he taught eighth grade physiology, sophomore geometry, freshman general science and junior-senior physics. The latter two subjects were taught in the basement, which he shared with the janitor, at Green Street. The ceiling of the basement was unfinished, so laboratory apparatus could be suspended by driving a nail into a rafter. As football and basketball coach, he convinced Mr. Jankers, owner of the Social Hall on York Road, that the auditorium at Green Street was insufficient for a winning basketball season. Mr. Jankers loaned the team the Social Hall, and teachers and players built protective screens for the hall's windows.

Referendums were held to build a new high school. There was some opposition, and one businessman remarked that the only time some of the farmers were seen in the village was when they came in to vote against a new school. Construction was begun at York Road and First Avenue in the summer of 1926. Fred Fenton became superintendent for District 100, as well as District 2, and continued in this dual role until his death in 1943.

In 1927, on what is recalled as a sunny afternoon, seventy-nine students of the Community High School, their parents, and teachers formed a parade down York Road from Green Street to the new school. They carried their books and personal belongings to deposit in their own individual lockers in the new building. In addition, the seventh and eighth grade students moved into the high school and received for the first time a fully depart-

Bensenville Community High School's first football team, 1926 Top row: Vernon Franzen, Orville Sizer, Charles Earhart, Tommy Kouzmanoff. Middle row: Steve Owens, Ed Gallery, Russell Morse, Roger Morse, Leonard Rasmussen. Bottom row: Reinie Eichleman, Eugene Gutnick, Wesley A. Johnson, Johnny Schoppe.

Bensenville Community High School's first basketball team 1926-1927
Front row: Vernon Franzen, Royal Kerch, Russell Morse, Fred
Koebbeman, Leonard Rasmussen. Second row: Charles Earhart,
Oliver Franzen, Steve Owens, Wesley A. Johnson.

mentalized program, including shop, homemaking, and
physical education.

Lynn Huffman became the band instructor and music
director in the fall of 1927. He was first employed on a part-
time basis by Districts 2 and 100, (and also taught in the
grade schools in Franklin Park.) In 1949, he became
supervisor of the music program and director on instru-
mental instruction for both 100 and 2, until his retirement
in 1962. Huffman Park on Church Road was named to
honor the musician for his work with the municipal band
and Bensenville's students.

In 1929, the District 2 board voted to buy the Tioga
School site from William F. Franzen for $6,576.20. Notices
of a special election were posted in public places..."on
Koelker's Store, at Olhaber's Store, the village hall, the
schoolhouse, Kerker's place on Irving Park and Marshall
Road, at Schmidt's Filling Station on Irving Park, the
high school, Volk Bros. on York, and the telephone pole
at Church Road and Third Avenue." On February 15,
1930, the vote to build Tioga was approved by the voters,
ninety to seventy-four.

TIOGA

Bensenville Community High School, built in 1927

Tioga School was opened in 1931, the lower six classrooms assigned to the upper grades. Green Street School became a lower elementary school building. By 1935, there were 545 children enrolled in the grade school, so it became necessary to finish two of the second floor classrooms. As the school enrollment grew, the rest of the building was finished.

On Mr. Fenton's death in 1943, Wesley A. Johnson was appointed superintendent of Districts 2 and 100. The population of the village had grown during the '40's and the schools were crowded. Green Street had to be divided into eight rooms to accommodate the first and second grades. Tioga was expanded in 1947 with the addition of a new wing. Parents had requested kindergarten classes in the fall of 1947, and Mrs. Gertrude Wooley conducted kindergarten for the district on a tuition basis for a year and two-thirds in the basement of the First E. U. B. Church on Lincoln Avenue. Upon completion of Tioga, tuition was eliminated and kindergarten became part of the school program.

KINDER-
GARTEN

A local postwar planning committee reporting to the Board of Education in 1945, pointed to the seating shortage

Aerial view of Bensenville, showing Tioga School and Bensenville Community High School

85

in the grade schools and recommended immediate plans be made for a new school building. The school tax levy was increased and Tioga School was enlarged. Green Street School was remodeled; the wide wooden stairways and wooden floors in the central hallways which were considered a fire hazard, were replaced by fireproof construction. A seven-room school was built to accommodate the children in the Mohawk subdivision. W. A. Johnson School was built in 1958 to serve the southwest part of the district.

A citizens' committee, under the direction of John Spence, John Green and Charles Ortega, approached the District 100 board to request that a new high school be built. The citizens' committee undertook to sell the proposition to the public, and on February 28, 1953, a special election was held to vote on the issuing of bonds to purchase a high school site. The public approved the $46,000 bond issue. The citizens' committee organized area directors and blockworkers to publicize the referendum of November 14, 1953, to issue $1,140,000 in bonds to build the new high school. This referendum also passed and ground was broken May 24, 1954, for Fenton High School. Grove Street was opened onto Route 83 to allow

Wesley A. Johnson, at the head of the table facing the camera, chairing the 1975 school history committee

the construction equipment to come into the site. The resulting white brick high school was one of the most attractive suburban schools built in the '50's, but the expensive white brick caused considerable criticism in Bensenville at the time. It has proved its worth, and subsequent additions to Fenton have utilized the same materials.

An issue of particular concern to the school boards in the '60's was of federal aid to education. Startled by Sputnik and the possibility that the American educational system was not as efficient as Russia's, citizens demanded new teaching programs and methods. Federal funding offered an opportunity for additional programs, but the school boards strongly objected to any possibility that federal money would mean federal control of the local school. Martin Romme recalls that this issue occupied many hours of the board's time, and three years brought about a reversal of opinion. Submitting to financial pressures, school boards availed themselves of federal funds. The dreaded interference did not materialize, and schools began actively seeking federal grants for title programs and school lunch programs.

A special election was required to allow District 100 to sell the Bensenville Community High School building on York Road to District 2. This became Blackhawk Junior High School and Mrs. Vivian Turner, who had been a principal at Green Street, Tioga, Johnson and Lincoln Schools, became the first Blackhawk principal. In the fall of 1965, Mrs. Turner and Blackhawk Junior High School moved into the new building on Church Road, and the York Road school became Chippewa Elementary School.

BLACKHAWK JUNIOR HIGH SCHOOL

In addition to the public school system, St. Alexis Church, St. Charles Borromeo Church, and Zion Evangelical Lutheran Church maintain elementary schools in Bensenville.

Fenton High School began enlarging in 1974. A new library, classrooms, field house, and an auditorium are being completed. The larger facility will enable the school schedule to return to a regular school day, accommodating the entire student body in the school at one time.

BENSENVILLE SCHOOL DIRECTORS AND SCHOOL DISTRICT 2 BOARD MEMBERS

George Cogswell	1885-1891
C. A. Franzen	1885-1892, 1900-1913
Herman H. Korthauer	1885-1893
A. D. Rotermund	1900-1906
Louis Brettman	1900-1906
J. C. Geils	1906-1922
H. L. Senne	1907-1921
C. E. Kirchoff	1914-1916
Fred Landmieir	1916-1922
Jessie O. Capoot	1922, 1928-1932
George Runge	1922-1936
Harry H. Geils	1922-1927
Carleton L. Brown	1922-1929
George F. Brentner	1922-1927
W. A. Ernsting	1922, 1928-1929
William F. Dunteman	1923-1928
Benjamin H. Schmidt	1923-1941
Herman Beyers	1923
Walter Olhaber	1924-1929
E. E. Bartholmey	1928-1932
Albert W. Franzen	1929-1932
August Freie	1930, 1933-1935
Alphonse P. Heim	1930-1947
J. G. Frey	1931-1940
William Bishop	1932-1941
Edwin H. Sprandel	1933-1950
John F. Thomas	1936-1939
Robert Oswald	1937-1940
J. W. Brown	1939-1951
David H. Rands	1940-1943
Elsworth R. Whitney	1940-1943, 1946-1951
W. H. Daly	1941-1945
D. J. Irvine	1941
Ronald Dettmann	1942-1945

Meredith E. Dobry	1943-1944
A. P. Stresen-Reuter	1943-1944
Arthur Peterson	1944-1948, 1951, 1960
A. J. Wagner	1944-1950
Leroy Raper	1944-1950
Robert E. Koehler	1948-1952
Peter M. Currie	1949-1950, 1952
George Adis	1949-1960
Clarence Van Dusen	1951-1961
Charles A. Lowe	1951-1954
Carl E. Wehr	1951-1966
Richard Daughtery	1952-1955
Thomas Simms	1953-1960
Anna C. Lirja	1954-1958
John Spence	1956-1965
Joy Barth	1957-1960
Martin I. Romme	1959-1971
Alfred W. Travers	1960-1966
James DiOrio	1961-1970
Paul G. Asgeirson	1961-1968
Thomas Barber	1965-1969
George Neilsen	1966-1969
Robert Townsend	1966-1969
Earl Meyer	1967-1968
Jean Blazek	1968-
Ray Basso	1969-1971
Will Davidson	1968-1969
Roy Tison	1969-1973, 1975-
Richard Whiting	1969-1971
Robert Broderick	1970-1974
Hartl R. Jones	1970-
Vick Johnson	1971-1975
John Curtis	1971-
Michael D. Murphy	1972-1975
Judith Ingram	1973-1976
Ken Frey	1974
John Orlyk	1975-
Edward Rossman	1975-

MEMBERS OF DISTRICT 100 SCHOOL BOARD

William F. Dunteman	1925-1934
Benjamin H. Schmidt	1925-1944
Harry H. Geils	1925-1927
Carleton L. Brown	1925-1928
Walter C. Olhaber	1925-1928
W. A. Ernsting	1927-1928
H. G. Franzen	1929-1933
J. O. Capoot	1930-1934
August Freie	1931-1934
James O'Keefe	1932-1933
Louis Cornille	1933-1945
Herman A. Dohe	1933-1935
Walter Lauman	1933-1937
Fred Koebbeman	1934-1938
William C. Krause	1936-1939
William Bishop	1936-1938, 1942-1950
Raymond Wilson	1939-1943
Julius G. Frey	1940-1943
Elmer Kurtz	1942-1957
William H. Daly	1943-1949
Clair Gerding	1944-1947
Ewald Lang	1944-1958
William Six	1947-1951
E. Cris Larson	1949-1952
Harold Keeling	1949-1965
Maurice Vick	1951-1958
Wilbur Burde	1952-1958
Gerald Capoot	1952-1961
Phillip A. Randell	1952-1953
Raymond Herness	1952-1961
Ernest H. Olson	1956-1966
John Green	1958-1964
Ellsworth Sachse	1958-1969

John E. King	1959-1963
Julia Wolters	1961-1967
Edward Gerrity	1962-1965
John Duerkop	1963-1969
Lawrence W. Reimer	1964-1970
William J. Rosner	1965-1966
Oscar Sahagun	1965-1969
Gerald Daly	1966-1967
Morton Wright	1966-1973
Arthur W. Richter	1967-1971
James DiOrio	1967-1971
Will Davidson	1969-1971
Jess Parrish	1969-1972
Martin Romme	1969-1971
Wilfred Prather	1970-1973
Ray Basso	1971-1976
Don Schwanz	1971-1974
George F. Moreth	1971-1972
Fred Wernicke	1971-1976
Robert Bender	1972-1976
Guyla Hunt	1973-1976
Robert Henderson	1973-1976
Joseph Owen	1973-1976
Gorden Ingram	1974-1976

SUPERINTENDENTS OF SCHOOL DISTRICTS 2 and 100

Fred C. Fenton	1922-1943
Wesley A. Johnson	1943-1964
Martin Zuckerman	1964-1970
James Coad	1971-

THE POLICE DEPARTMENT

Ordinance No. 4, passed by the village board on July 26, 1884, created the office of the village marshal. Frank L. Ort was appointed marshal the following February. He was to keep the town free of tramps and at one time was to offer food and lodging at a cost not to exceed twenty-five cents a night to such strangers as found themselves stranded within the village limits after dark. A calaboose (which was also used for some fire apparatus) was built between Center and Addison Streets near Roosevelt. Some concern was expressed by the village board for heat in the building, and the village's stove was moved from the Gilde Hall to the calaboose in 1902. Meals for the occupants of the calaboose were provided by the wives of the marshals, or someone willing to earn extra money for cooking. It is doubtful men were kept long in jail in Bensenville. Prisoners were taken to Wheaton, if they were to be incarcerated for any period of time.

Night watchers were apparently required in the 1890's but the record doesn't say what they looked for or guarded. Later, the vandalism to the depot caused the officials of the Milwaukee Road to send critical letters to the village board, who replied they would do the best they could with the men available, but if the railroad expected better supervision of the depot, they should provide funds to hire extra men.

The salary of the marshal began at fifteen dollars a year in 1887. In 1894, the marshal was to be paid ten cents for each tramp he locked up. In 1913, Albert Raack was appointed village marshal and requested $100 a year salary. The following month, Henry Marshall received the appointment.

Bensenville had police magistrates, who apparently held court to hear cases of minor infractions of the law and to collect fines. When the village hall was built in 1908, jail cells were constructed on the ground level. Eventually the police radio was installed there also.

It was felt necessary, in 1921, for the board to order that the village marshal should not take orders from anyone but the village president or the board of trustees. The problems of law and order in farming communities were not felt to be severe enough to require a large police force, so for many years, one or two men at a time kept the peace. By 1941, provision was made for special policemen to help the chief several hours a month. The village population had increased during the war, and as local customs and moral values had changed, police work increased. In 1956, Bensenville's police department came under the civil service laws. The referendum creating a Fire and Police Commission created a local board responsible for the personnel of the police and fire departments. This commission must publish the schedule of examinations for positions in the departments in newspapers throughout the Chicago area. Candidates are given a physical agility test, a written exam designed and graded by the Illinois Testing Bureau, and an oral interview by the Commission. If these tests are passed, the candidate must take an in-depth psychological test, a physical, and a polygraph exam. When these tests are successfully passed, the name of the candidate is referred to the village board for appointment to fill vacancies in the departments. The Commission also arbitrates personnel problems and investigates complaints.

CIVIL SERVICE

Patrol car radio communication systems had not been developed. A Bensenville resident requiring the assistance of the police called the local telephone operator. She would turn on the red light atop the water tower to alert the policeman in the squad car. He would then stop at the nearest phone and call the operator to find out who needed his help.

Former Police Chief Walter Tett recalls that in 1954, there was only one squad car for the village with a population of 3,700. A new patrolman received no training or testing. He was handed the keys and told to go to work. There was no overtime pay, and the days off were usually Wednesday or Thursday. The department was primarily concerned with traffic control and deterring burglaries. By 1960, the appropriation for the police department was $84,000, and eleven men were employed. Much of the work still involved traffic, but juvenile and domestic problems were a growing concern. The department developed a program of community relations with talks to parent groups and school visits.

CADET
PROGRAM

The cadet program, begun in 1970, gave a young man an opportunity to try police work as a career. It was necessary to be a high school graduate and between seventeen and nineteen years of age; the cadet then worked with the police department under the direction of the chief. By the age of twenty-one, the patrolman exam had to be taken. If this exam was passed, the candidate was put on the list for recommended employment. If the exam was failed, the cadet was required to relinquish the job. Cadets usually supplemented the on-job-training with courses at the College of DuPage or Triton College.

In 1972, the new public safety building was dedicated on North Church Road by Illinois Governor Ogilvie. Built with the aid of a grant of $117,370 from the Illinois Law Enforcement Commission, the new building provided facilities for offices, labs, records, and detention cells.

PUBLIC
SERVICE
BUILDING

The station was staffed twenty-four hours a day, and squad cars placed on the streets of the village around the clock. The major concern was still traffic problems, but as the population increased, police work increased. The detective, juvenile and narcotics divisions became specialized. As in all other aspects of municipal government, the trend was towards professionalism in the police field.

Stanley D. Troyer was appointed police chief in 1975. Following the trend toward professionalism in municipal government, Chief Troyer has twenty years of police experience and a Master's Degree in Police Science. The department has a staff of thirty-three and a 1976 budget of $668,887.

VILLAGE MARSHALS AND CHIEFS OF POLICE

Marshals

Frank L. Ort	1885
Charles Sandhagen	1886
Otto Koch	1892
Charles Martin	1893
Alexander Schmidt	1894
Conrad Schneider	1896
August Kraegel	1898
Herman Baucke	1903
Henry Holt	1908
Herman Brettman	1910
Albert Raack	1913
Henry Marshall	1913

Chief of Police

Charles Irwin	1929
John Frost	1930
Honus Wagner	1933
Ralph Corrigan	1939
Robert E. Carr	1940
Melbourne E. Matsen	1941
James Venner	1942
Harold Mack	1944
Harry Kolze	1947
Walter E. Tett	1961
Stanley Troyer	1975

THE FIRE DEPARTMENT

In 1890 or 1891, a picnic was held in Bensenville to raise money for a small hand-operated fire engine. The equipment was used to fight fires at the Runge barn, the Bensenville Depot, and the Koehn barn. These structures were not saved, but the adjacent buildings were. It was apparent that trained fire fighters were required. On August 27, 1894, the Bensenville Volunteer Fire Department was organized with 21 charter members. The first meetings were held in rooms above Tiedemann's Store. Herman H. Korthauer was elected chief, Charles Martin, assistant chief, Frederick H. Wolkenhauer, engineer, Fred Elfring, secretary, and William L. Korthauer, treasurer. A constitution and bylaws were adopted. The following month, the first fire department picnic was held to raise money for equipment. The concessions included a wheel of fortune, a bar, and stands selling baby dolls, canes, and candy. The profit of $74.89 was sufficient to buy a hose-drying rack, raincoats for each member, and a padlock for the engine house with three dozen keys.

Frederick Wolkenhauer made a firebell of two triangular pieces of iron hung about nine inches apart, which gave the effect of a bell ringing when struck together. This bell was hung in a tower on the icehouse near Tiedemann's Store. Chief Korthauer ordered the bell rung continuously

Hand pumper, of the same type owned by the Bensenville Volunteer
Fire Department

and as loudly as possible for a fire. It was rung twice,
stopped, rung twice, stopped, and repeated for a fire drill.
The members of the fire department would leave their work
and race to the firehouse on hearing the bell. All the well
and cisterns in town were inspected and their location
noted. In the event of fire, the cisterns were used as a
source of water. The department investigated the possibility
of building a ten barrel wooden tank on the old engine
truck to be able to carry water to the fire.

The following year, the second fund raising picnic was
held in Korthauer's Pine Grove on Park Street. A dance
floor was built for the occasion and Japanese lanterns hung
in the trees. An outdoor bowling alley was constructed.
The pins and balls were kept in a box at the grove and
served to entertain groups for a number of years. The
1896 picnic proceeds were used to purchase uniforms for
all the members.

The men of Bensenville volunteered to be members of the
department and were voted in by the membership.
Originally, they were not paid for fire fighting. The chief
and other officers were elected by the members, and the

First photo of the Bensenville Volunteer Fire Department, on Main Street in front of C. A. Franzen's house in 1895. Fire Chief Herman H. Korthauer is standing to the left of the front row.

results of these elections were passed on to the village board, who extended their customary approval. The duties of various positions of responsibility were set forth in the 1899 Fire Department Constitution and Bylaws. The chief was to go directly to the fire and decide how best it be fought, where the engine should be set, and check the nearest water supply. The assistant chief was to go to the engine house and see that the tank on the fire engine was charged with water and that it started to the fire as quickly as possible. He was also directed to precede the engine to the fire, pick out the road for it, and carry a lantern at night. The engineer had general supervision of the engine and was responsible for putting chemical in the tank and having it in good operating condition. The hose captain had charge of the hose and cart, and the hook and ladder captain had charge of the hook and ladder truck and the men assigned to it. The pumper was drawn by horses, often the nearest team was pressed into service to pull the engine to the fire. The chief was empowered to command the services of any bystander to help fight the fire.

The fire department was trained and available, and so ministered to most local emergencies and tragedies. The organization was strong, close and proud, and very practical, and through the years developed into an efficient modern organization. New equipment was acquired as quickly as possible and new fire fighting techniques adopted.

In 1895, the fire engine house was located at the alley facing Roosevelt Avenue between Center and Addison. The village board ordered the firehouse lined, as it must have been quite cold. Three years later, the engine house was located on Schwerdtfeger's property at the southeast corner of Green and Center.

In 1903, a bell tower was erected on railroad property on the east side of Center Street. The department had been meeting at the Gilde Hall, but they were forced to find new quarters when it burned October 30, 1903. When the new village hall was completed at York and Railroad, the fire engine and all the apparatus were moved to

In 1896 The Fire Department purchased uniforms for all the members. The team of horses belonged to Henry Thieman, who is holding the reins.

the new engine room on July 5, 1909. In 1922, the first motorized Reo, a combination pumper and ladder truck, was bought. An electric alarm system was installed and in 1930, a new fire siren was added to the bell tower.

A request was made to the village board by the fire department in 1926 that the firemen be paid for fighting fires. "In the past, we have been willing to give our services voluntarily, on account of the village being small and fires less frequent than they are at the present time, but now we feel the village large enough to create a fund which would take care of compensation of the men on duty." The village board decided that the fireman should be paid two dollars for the first hour and one dollar each extra hour for reporting to a fire. Each man was to be paid two dollars per drill. The volunteers turned most of their pay back into the organization to pay for the department's fire fighting equipment.

The village board ordered the fire department in 1937 not to take the equipment out of the village limits and leave the residents of Bensenville unprotected. A few weeks later, a house burned at the edge of the village, killing two children. The fire department went to the fire having decided that the order could be broken, but nothing could be done to save the children. In order to prevent a recurrence of this tragedy, the Rural Fire Protection League was organized. The volunteers who made up this group were residents of the unincorporated areas around the village responsible for fighting fires outside the village limits. The chief of the Bensenville Volunteer Fire Department was chief of the Rural Fire Protection League also. The money which was raised at the carnivals was evenly divided between the two departments to buy equipment for their own needs. A 500 gallon pumper and ladder combination with a 450 gallon booster tank was purchased for the rural firemen's use. The old engine house was too small to house this truck, so the firemen spent several weekends enlarging the building. Proceeds from the carnivals were set aside to build a new fire station.

RURAL FIRE PROTECTION LEAGUE

Fire bell tower behind the Village Hall in the 1930's. The electric siren was added in 1930.

Original fire bell, purchased in 1905, which hung at Center Street and Railroad Avenue.

Fire equipment and the Fire House at 15 N. York were financed by dances, picnics, and carnivals sponsored by the Volunteer Fire Department. Seated in a 1926 Lincoln are Bill Grobe, Bill Feiler, Al Mahler, Harry Kolze, George Korthauer, George Boldebuck and Herb Grishow. Standing on the right is Paul Luessenhop.

Bensenville Volunteer Fire Department, May 30, 1949, on the site of the future fire hall which they built at 15 N. York Road.

In 1949, the village and rural departments were combined to form the Bensenville Firemen's Association. The fire station at 15 North York was begun in 1950. Financed, planned, and owned by the firemen themselves, it provided storage for the equipment and apparatus, kitchen facilities, and a large hall which was available for rent and served as a congregating place for the firemen's social activities.

Bensenville's fire department has fought several large fires. In 1945, spontaneous combustion ignited the Milwaukee Road coal chute near the roundhouse about 5 a.m., on a cold November morning. The roof, 150 feet from the ground, was enveloped in flames when the fire department arrived. Hoses had to be laid atop nearby towers to reach above the burning roof, and the firemen had to chop through four inch planking to reach the burning coal inside the chute. They worked ten hours in cold wet weather to put out the fire and save the coal chute.

On Sunday, September 17, 1961, an airliner crashed near Irving Park Road, one minute after takeoff from O'Hare Field. The plane hit a 34,000 volt power line, struck a railroad embankment, and burst into flames.

Farm house at 101 N. Church Road was burned in November 1956 in a training exercise for the Fire Department.

The Bensenville Fire Department arrived at the crash, which was in the southwest corner of the airport, ten minutes before any other equipment appeared. The pumpers carrying water were immediately used to put water on the burning tail section. The plane exploded twice while the firemen were attempting to put out the fire, and only when it was evident that all aboard were dead, did the firemen retreat from the flames. The Bensenville Fire Department was commended by a resolution in the Illinois House of Representatives for its efficiency in the emergency. Since that crash, Chicago and most suburban departments have adopted combination tank and pumper equipment, which is capable of carrying water to the fire.

Two spectacular and dangerous fires were fought in 1963. On July 5, the building which had housed the hardware store in which the village had been incorporated in 1884, burst into flames. Ellmore's Flower Shop, the Main Liquor Store, Eleanor's Bake Shop, and Sport-N-Work Clothing Store were destroyed. The old building had been rebuilt several times and there were no fire walls separating the units. The combination of bake ovens, liquor, and flammable goods produced flames which could be seen for miles. At one point, the front window blew out, throwing glass across Main Street onto the Milwaukee tracks. Michael A. Kudelas' house on Center Street was so close to the fire that firemen had to turn sideways to get between the two buildings. However, the Kudelas home was protected from damage by a foam spray. Forty-seven men from Bensenville, Wood Dale, and Addison fought the fire for five hours.

A month later on August 9, 1963, the townhouses under construction on Hamilton Street caught fire. The buildings were quite close together, and the fire spread from one unfinished building to another, so that the firemen were fighting a fire from both sides. One building collapsed, falling away from the firemen. Volunteer fireman Horace Langguth did not report back to the firehouse. He was found near the burned out area, his death attributed to a heart attack following his exertion fighting the fire.

George Korthauer, Sr., retired in 1967 after serving fifty-two years in the department, thirty-one years as chief. Armin Korthauer, his brother, succeeded him as chief. Originally a volunteer department supported by donations, the fire department had become a tax supported body as a part of the fire protection district and function of the village government. From hand-drawn pumpers, the department had developed modern techniques of fire fighting with new equipment they had helped design to fit their needs.

Martin Heinrich was appointed the first full-time fire chief under the civil service laws in 1970. Willard Schoppe was appointed full-time assistant fire chief. There are six full-time fire department members and 29 volunteers. A year's training program by the department prepares the volunteers to serve as firemen. Chief Heinrich states that the department relies on volunteers, and their training must be in all phases of fire service before they can answer fire calls.

The Milwaukee roundhouse fire, in the early 1970's, involved the Bensenville Fire Department and departments from six other towns. Flammable materials stored in the roundhouse fed the flames of the wooden structure. The fire loss to the railroad was set at $500,000. Shortly afterwards, the American Furnace Company factory burned in a large difficult fire at a loss of $400,000. The Greek Orthodox Church, which had been the Immanuel Church built in 1924, burned in September of 1972, probably ignited by candles used in a Saturday morning service. Within a month, the fire department fought a house fire in the unincorporated area. Flames pouring out a window were seen by people going by in the early morning. The fire department found a difficult fire well established by the time they were called, but the occupant and the house were saved.

The current equipment of the Bensenville Fire Department includes four pumpers, an eighty-five foot aerial tower, three cars (one of which carries inhalator equipment),

Bensenville Firemen's Association 1954. 1st row: Joseph Chabin, Rudy Laho, Ed Mahler, Harry Kolze, Roy Imwie, Jerry Goble, Walter Olhaber. 2nd row: John Geils, Herb Grishow, Harold Runge, Dayton McIntyre, Delbert Kolze, Irn Leubking, Martin Heinrich. 3rd row: Walter Kehoe, Al Kolze, George Korthauer, Armin Korthauer, Arnold Grobe, Ed Heinrich.

Four Chiefs of the Bensenville Fire Department at the dedication of the new fire station on South York Road June 1972. Left to right: George Boldebuck, George Korthauer, Armin Korthauer, and the present chief, Martin Heinrich.

a 2,000 gallon tanker and a squad truck. The fire district the Bensenville Fire Department serves comprises ten square miles. The department still maintains equipment that will carry water to a fire, because some areas of the district do not have fireplugs.

MEMBERSHIP ROLL
BENSENVILLE FIRE DEPARTMENT

Herman H. Korthauer	1894-1930
Fred Elfring	1894-1896
Charles Wellner	1894-1896
Charles E. Martin	1894-1898
William L. Korthauer	1894-1896
Fred Koelker	1894-1931
Dick Cieszinsky	1894-1896
Frank Steiglider	1894-1896
Fred H. Volberding	1894-1942
H. F. Sandhagen	1894-1903
J. T. Tiedemann	1894-1933
Julius Baucke	1894-1895
Ernst Boldebuck	1894-1937
John Huber	1894-1900
Alex Schmidt	1894-1896
F. J. Mess	1894-1911
Henry Lagerhausen	1894-1896
Emil Ott	1894-1896
F. H. Wolkenhauer	1894-1926
J. C. Geils	1894-1916
Fritz Kropp	1894-1896
Herman Baucke	1895-1903
Theodore Kock	1895-1896
Fred Greinke	1895-1898
Herman Schmoldt	1895
Henry Thieman	1895-1910
August Schwerdtfeger	1895-1915
Ed Winkelman	1896
Gustav Gutsche	1896-1918
Fred Schmidt	1896-1898
H. Finke	1896-1897

Fred Warnecke	1896-1903
H. L. Geils	1896
H. B. Marshall	1897-1930
L. Moss	1897-1898
George E. Franzen	1897-1926
August Freie	1898-1907
Charles Olhaber	1899-1925
George Struckman	1899-1903
Louis Brettman	1899-1919
John Schwass	1899-1900
Ed Freie	1900-1912
Henry Sprandel	1900
R. Schmoldt	1900
W. F. Dunteman	1902-1938
Carl Kirchoff	1903-1938
Ernst Schultz	1903-1913
Louis Grobe	1903-1935
John Schaettler	1903-1912
Louis Schroeder	1905-1908
Victor Beck	1907-1926
Ernst Stelkopf	1909-1920
William Grobe	1911-1948
Robert Pilgrim	1911-1942
George Runge	1913-1946
Albert Raack	1913-1926
Henry Holt	1914-1950
Louis Blume	1914-1917
George L. Korthauer	1915-1967
William Urban	1915-1918
Fred Ahlborn	1915-1935
Charles Perlberg	1915-1925
Joseph J. Jankers	1915-1916
Herman C. Brettman	1915-1917
Harry Geils	1915-1933
Herman Kossacks	1917-1920
E. J. Franzen	1918-1950
Dr. I. W. Riggens	1920
Harry Franzen	1920-1928
George Boldebuck	1920-1947

Otto Herrs	1920-1937
Harry Kolze	1920-1954
William Ernsting	1921-1946
Herman Wagner	1921-1935
Alwin Mahler	1921-1961
Julius G. Frey	1922-1947
Herman Beyers	1922
Otto Grobe	1929-1936
W. C. Olhaber	1929-1969
Albert Kolze	1930-1973
Armin Korthauer	1935-1970
Vernon Franzen	1936-1951
Walter Lauman	1937-1953
Arthur Seiber	1937-1939, 1948-1950, 1957-1961
Fred Koebbeman	1937-1943
Albert Born	1937-1951
Arnold Grobe	1938-1958
Wilbur Shebeck	1941-1945
Martin Westby	1942-1947
Cecil Poor	1942-1946
Ed Heinrich	1943-1963
George Grobe	1943-1948
Rudolph Laho, Jr.	1945-1968
Joseph Chaban, Jr.	1946-1948
Ed Jorns	1947-1968
William Webb	1947-1950
Walter Kehoe	1947-1975
Dayton McIntyre	1948-1963
John Spanley	1948-1952
Marvin Rusteberg	1948-1974
John Geils	1950-1963
Roy Imwie	1950-1954
Harold Runge	1950-1970
Erwin Luebking, Jr.	1951-1957, 1959-1968
Martin Heinrich	1951-
Gerold Goble	1952-1975

Delbert Kolze	1952-1971
Herbert Grischow	1952-1960
Joseph Chaban	1952-1954
John Berry	1955-1966
Robert Standard	1955-1972
Allen Kissane	1955-1972
Charles Jones	1955-1957
Edwin Piepenbrink	1955-
Clarence Wilkie	1955-1959
Robert Geils	1956-1961
Willard Schoppe	1957-
Frank Gough	1957-1972
Horace Langguth	1958-1963
Richard Thomas	1959-1965
Leonard Malina	1959-1963
Fred Sieber	1960-1974
Harold Marshall	1961-1972
James Ehrhardt	1961-1973
Bert Severson	1961-1969
Joseph Martyniuk	1961-
William Keller, Jr.	1961-1970
John Lill	1963-1974
Albert Richert	1963-
Steve Heike	1963-1971
James Garry	1963-
Dean Hammersley	1963-1966
Charles Simon	1963-
George Freda	1966-
William Heinrich	1966-
Al Quinn	1968-1973
Norman Thompson	1968-
Herbert Hasse	1969-1970
Gregory DuPre	1970-
Kenneth Majeska	1970-1973
Thomas Flanagan	1970
Gerald Seiden	1971-
Chester Luby	1971-
Bernard McCauley	1971-
James Dena	1971-

Rick D. Willey	1972-
Daniel Jackson	1972-
Scott Ingebrigtsen	1972-1974
Stanley Jakalski	1973
Mitchel Srail	1973-
Leonard Swintek	1973-
Raymond Batista	1973-
Joseph Albert	1973-
John Kreft	1973-
Thomas Ryan	1974-
William Barr	1974-
Michael Puntillo	1974-
Rick Furgiuele	1974-
Ronald Schultz	1974-
Edward Joncours	1975-
Ronnie Gough	1975-
Kevin Brennan	1975-
Anthony Scandora	1975-
Lawrence Kochan	1975-

CHIEFS OF THE
BENSENVILLE FIRE DEPARTMENT

Herman H. Korthauer	1894-1903
E. M. Boldebuck	1903-1912
Herman H. Korthauer	1912-1915
George Runge	1915-1916
E. M. Boldebuck	1916-1919
Louis Grobe	1919-1922
George Korthauer	1922-1924
E. M. Boldebuck	1924-1928
George Korthauer	1928-1936
George Boldebuck	1936-1947
George Korthauer	1947-1967
Armin Korthauer	1967-1970
Martin Heinrich	1970-

THE PARK DISTRICT

In the fall of 1959, the Greater Bensenville Recreation Association had not received enough funding in its four years of operation of the pool to improve the area now known as Veterans Park. The growing need for athletic programs for boys and girls in the community required financial support. Village President Gust Van Mol recognizing the limitations of village funds for parks and recreational purposes called a public meeting which included members of the Illinois Association of Park Districts to discuss various methods of securing local tax support. It was decided to study the feasibility of organizing a special taxing district, separate and independent of the Village of Bensenville, for the purpose of providing parks and recreation activities.

After numerous civic and neighborhood meetings, the study committee chaired by William Grothstruck and Robert Nichols, recommended a park district be formed. A referendum supervised by Village Attorney William A. Redmond was held August 17, 1960; the vote for the formation of the park district was 444 in favor to 332 against. Five of the ten candidates were elected commissioners: Rudolph H. Krempels, Wayne H. Scheppele, Robert S. Nichols, John D. Varble, and Maxine L. Geils. Robert Nichols was selected the first president, and Maxine Geils the first secretary-treasurer.

FORMATION OF PARK DISTRICT

The boundaries of the newly formed district were Devon Avenue to the north; the Chicago and Northwestern Railroad to the east including a portion of Cook County; Mount Emblem Cemetery, Grand Avenue, and Belmont Avenue to the south; and the boundaries of School District 2 on the west to Wood Dale Road to Route 83 and Devon. The first tax funds were received in the spring of 1961, and by fall improvements were being made in existing parks. Krempels, Rose, Seekarr, Sunset, and Veterans parks were owned by the village and later deeded to the park district. The land under the swimming pool was held by the village to honor a lease with the Greater Bensenville Recreation Association.

LAND PURCHASES

The first land purchased by the park district was along Route 83 in 1962. This 2.8 acre parcel became the west side of Varble Park. Lands leased from School District 2 and the ball fields used by the Bensenville Boys Athletic Association were maintained by the park district for spring and summer activities. Most of the park district's early funds were spent in improvements and development at Veterans Park.

The locomotive monument at Veterans Park was donated by a group of concerned citizens. In 1964, the Bensenville Junction Miniature Golf Course was constructed becoming the park district's first revenue facility. Each year, the park district assumed more direct support and supervision of the revenue pool operation.

An additional 18.1 acres were purchased in 1965 from the DuPage County Forest Preserve District to form the east side of Varble Park. In the spring of 1966, the park district's first capital program was begun to provide additions to the north and south of the Community Building at Veterans Park, the purchase of the Greater Bensenville Association's rights to the Richard D. Thomas Memorial Pool, and an option to purchase White Pines Golf Course. Promised federal matching funds to purchase the White Pines Golf Course were cancelled. However, the park district board was able to sell $1,680,000 in revenue bonds to finance the purchase of the course and the sale was

White Pines Golf Course

completed in the fall of 1967. Final monies of the 1967 bond issue were received in August of 1969 and used to purchase the center six acres of Varble Park. Poplar Park and the land which linked DuPage Forest Preserve property leased by the park district on the west were also purchased with these funds.

The first tax money to be used specifically for recreation purposes was received in 1970. The development of a complete recreation program meant greater service to the residents of the Bensenville Park District.

In January of 1972, the park district assumed direct management of White Pines Golf Course from the Branigar Organization which had managed the course for the district. By summer of 1972, the purchase of Sunrise Park was completed. In 1973, Lions Park was deeded to the park district by the joint action of the Bensenville Lions Club and the village.

The Bensenville Park District has a population of 19,000 residents. Approximately fifty acres of land are available in neighborhood parks and 260 acres comprise the White Pines Golf Course. White Pines revenue bonds have several years to go, but the necessary reserves have been paid and

117

John H. Franzen's Flax seed grinding stones

Bensenville Park District's summer playground program

the district has funds available for course improvements. In 1975, voters approved the purchase of a portion of the St. Alexis Church property which contains the ball fields used by the Bensenville Boys Athletic Association. In 1975, Sunrise, Rose, Poplar, and Varble parks were developed, and tennis courts were built at Sunset and Sunrise.

Funds to operate and maintain the park district are derived from a general tax which produced $125,000, and a recreation tax which produced $92,000 in 1975. The current White Pines Golf Course budget approaches $820,000. In 1976, the district has a current total budget of over $1 million compared to just $33,000 in 1961.

The Bensenville Park District has a professional director. Dan Plaza came from Sunnyvale, California, in 1970, with a Master's Degree in Park and Recreation Administration to oversee the operation of the district. The district employes twenty full-time persons and over 200 part-time staff members on a seasonal basis. The growth and development of the Bensenville Park District is a source of pride to the residents, the staff, and the Board of Commissioners.

PRESIDENTS
BENSENVILLE PARK DISTRICT

Robert S. Nichols	1960-1963
John D. Varble	1963-1965
Wayne H. Scheppele	1965-1966
John D. Varble	1966-1968
John W. Schuster	1968-1969
Donald E. Carroll	1969-1970
Wilbur C. Burde	1970-1971
Robert S. Nichols	1971
John W. Schuster	1971-1973
John J. Piegore	1973-1974
John J. Gianforte	1974

BOARD OF COMMISSIONERS
BENSENVILLE PARK DISTRICT

Rudolph H. Krempels	1960-1966
Wayne H. Scheppele	1960-1965
Robert S. Nichols	1960-1973
John D. Varble	1960-1969
Maxine L. Geils	1960-1963
John W. Schuster	1963-1974
Wilbur C. Burde	1965-1971
Donald E. Carroll	1965-1972
Merle K. Hummell	1969-1971
John J. Piegore	1971-
John J. Gianforte	1971-
Ricardo E. Guzman	1972-1974
John R. Schrimpl	1973-1974
Robert S. Nichols	1974-
Charles K. Whitaker	1974-
Hugg M. Holmes	1974-1975
Caralyn M. Kempa	1975-

THE LIBRARY

In March of 1956, a group of people interested in establishing a public library in Bensenville met to organize themselves into a committee. Wayne Schepple was elected chairman, and Mrs. Walter Baran was elected secretary-treasurer. The boundaries of the library district were to be those of School District 100, which would include the villages of Bensenville and Wood Dale. Residents were asked to donate books to establish a library collection. The new school library at Fenton offered shelf space for a cooperative adult library. Local organizations gave cash donations which purchased cataloging supplies, and a group of volunteers were trained to help with circulation. The library was open from six to nine p.m., on Tuesdays and Thursdays. A two dollar charge was made for membership in the library.

A library board was developed in 1958 with Clarence Thiemann, who had set up army libraries during World War II, as the first president. Later in 1958, the board reorganized into two districts, when Wood Dale decided to begin its own library. The Fenton space was inadequate for a public library, and the school library was growing. So the board asked the village for space and money. The Kolze farm had just been purchased by the village, and the farmhouse on the southwest corner of Irving Park and

FIRST
BOARD

121

Church Road was sound. The village reinforced the floors to support the weight of 3,000 books and purchased shelves, desks, a typewriter, tables, and chairs. It was rented to the library for one dollar per year. The Bensenville Jaycees washed walls, painted, and sanded woodwork. The library opened in January of 1960 with 3,000 books, one-third of them on loan from the Illinois Library Service Center.

LIBRARY DISTRICT FORMED

Public support in the form of tax money was necessary to maintain library services, so a referendum was held in May, 1960, to establish a public library district. Virginia Northrop recalls that many of the laws governing district libraries were obsolete. It was discovered that the "treasurer of the county would be the treasurer of the library district." This was somewhat of a surprise to the DuPage County treasurer, who nevertheless came to the Bensenville library board meetings to help determine procedures. William A. Redmond, the library attorney and a member of the state legislature was helpful in designing legislation which enabled district libraries to function. Bensenville pioneered in the growth of postwar district libraries. It took hours of volunteer time in board meetings that lasted far into the night, and days were spent sorting, moving, shelving books, and staffing a library.

FIRST LIBRARY

Dorothea Schmidt was appointed the first full-time librarian in July, 1961. With many years experience as director of a branch of the Chicago Library System, she found true adventure in Bensenville. The adult fiction collection was housed in the basement of the farmhouse, through the kitchen, and down the stairs. This lower level was immaculately neat; the floor shone and the walls were painted. According to local custom, the basement flooded during a prolonged wet spell. Miss Schmidt took administrative measures to correct that problem, and it did not flood again. The tiny kitchen served as the technical processing room. Books were unpacked, cataloged, covered, and marked on the kitchen counter, while library patrons marched back and forth on their way to the adult collection. Bensenville had few quiet restaurants where the library staff could have a quick lunch, so the staff set aside an area downstairs, and brought lunch from home. Miss Schmidt established the basic structure of the catalog and the collection, trained the staff, and began the community services programs that characterize a modern library.

Kolze's farmhouse was to be the site of Bensenville's new village hall, so the library had to move. The library board tried twice in 1964 to pass referendums to build a library building. The first plan was to build in Deer Park, but the proposal was defeated. A less expensive library was proposed for Lions Park, but that, too, was voted down. By 1964, taxpayers were feeling the pinch of new schools, new churches, and new libraries. The Branigar Real Estate office on the opposite corner of Church and Irving Park was for sale, and the library board was able to purchase it without a referendum.

The real estate office offered more room than the library had ever had, but it soon outgrew it. Two prefabricated buildings were added, providing a children's library wing and a reference room. Office space was added also. Art shows, adult book discussion groups, children's story hours, and increased library collections filled the library, and space again became a problem. In 1975, a referendum to build a new library at Plentywood failed. The library board opened a community center on Green Street at Addison to house theater group presentations, concerts, young people's and senior citizens' activities, and a collection of music, paperbacks, and games. The library's philosophy of service has caused it to be one of the most active institutions in Bensenville.

LIBRARIANS
BENSENVILLE COMMUNITY PUBLIC LIBRARY

Dorothea Schmidt	1961-1967
Dorothea Holland	1968-1971
Richard Thompson	1971-1974
Mary Anne Hamilton	1974-1975
William Schell	1975-

MEMBERS OF THE BOARD OF THE
BENSENVILLE COMMUNITY PUBLIC LIBRARY

Clarence Thiemann	1958-1963
Carol Weir	1958-1968
Virginia Northrop	1958-1968
Phyliss Spence	1958-1962
Mrs. Walter Baran, Sr.	1958-1960
George Moreth	1960-1964
Geraldine B. Sahagun	1962-1965
Dr. Martin Zuckerman	1964-1966
Thomas Wiley	1962-1963
Milford Bonner	1964-1966
Maurice R. Vick	1964-1970
Jacqueline C. Hack	1966-
Martha Chavance	1966-1971
Raymond Kielma	1966-1971
Beulah Baader	1968-1973
Kenneth Kaufman	1969-
Howard Hamilton	1970-
Ted Malin	1970-1971
Terrence Moreth	1972-1975
Lawrence J. Benac	1972
Donald Pieper	1972-1973
Wesley Poor	1973-
Dorothy McCabe	1974-
Gene O'Brien	1974-
Sal Bisceglie	1975-

THE CHURCHES

As early as 1837, church services were held in a small loghouse on Louis Schmidt's farm at the south end of Dunklee's Grove. This area came to be called Churchville from the two churches that still stand. L. C. Ervenberg, also called Ludwig Cachand, taught and preached in a building where the Schmidt house now stands. In 1840, Franz Hoffman came from Chicago and stayed three years, interrupting his ministry for a time to leave the area. The pulpit was supplied during his absence by a Methodist grocer from Chicago, who went back to his grocery when Hoffman returned in 1843. In 1847, the Rev. E. A. Brauer came to the church, which was then organized as the German Evangelical Lutheran Church. This group purchased forty-eight acres from Louis Schmidt for two hundred dollars on the east side of Church Road near Grand Avenue. The members of this congregation who had come from Hanover were Lutherans, and the families that had come from Prussia were of the Reformed faith. In 1848, the Reformed members severed their connections with this church and organized the Evangelical St. Johanne's Society. Two splits in the original congregation would give new churches to Bensenville. As the population increased in Addison Township, Zion would develop congregations in the new areas, which would become churches. A frame church was built on the east side of Church Road and eventually a bell tower was added. In 1862, the present yellow brick church and one hundred fifty foot steeple was built and dedicated. The present parsonage was built in 1872. Zion's cemetery dates from 1844. Zion Evangelical Lutheran Church has been the landmark for the Bensenville area for over one hundred thirty years, but had always stood outside the village. In 1976, in celebration of the nation's bicentennial, Zion was annexed to the village of Bensenville.

ST. JOHN'S

The Evangelical St. Johanne's Society received one hundred seventy dollars from the old Zion Church in return for former contributions to the Lutheran congregation, and sixty-five dollars for their share of the property. St. John's Church was built on Section 12, north of Bensenville, in the winter of 1849-50. Located on fourteen acres at Lawrence Avenue and Mt. Prospect Roads, this church served the residents of the surrounding farm community.

In 1951, the church was forced to move by the expansion of O'Hare Field, and the property was sold. The church was placed on wheels and was to be moved December 18, 1951. A big snow storm prevented the journey, and Christmas Eve services were held in the building as it stood on the wheels, with the congregation's cars parked beneath it. It took three weeks to move the church to the new site on Route 83. Pastor Bergstraesser recalls looking out his parsonage window at night to see the church standing out in the farmland to the west, and praying that the building would survive the journey. The parsonage was moved also, having been cut into two pieces for transporting. The move was completed in February, 1952. St. John's Cemetery remains on O'Hare property.

IMMANUEL CHURCH

The second split in the original Lutheran church established at the south end of Dunklee's Grove occurred in 1859, when the Immanuel Congregation was organized with Henry Fischer, Henry Buchholtz, and Frederick Schmidt as trustees, and the Rev. Carl Haass as the first pastor. The first Immanuel Church was built on the west side of Church Road on land donated by August Fischer.

Zion Lutheran Church built in 1862

St. John's United Church of Christ on Route 83, which was moved from O'Hare Field in 1951

Immanuel Church, 1860

A gothic frame structure with a tower and steeple was dedicated in 1860. Until 1925, only German services were held.

The Churchville schoolhouse, originally a church related school, was built in 1866. Fire destroyed the frame church building in 1924, but by May of that year, construction was begun by Ehlers Brothers for a brick church on the same site. It was dedicated in April, 1925. By 1958, Immanuel had outgrown this building, and an educational building was built on the east side of Church Road. In 1966, a new church was built on the east side of Church to the north of the educational wing. The 1925 church was destroyed by fire and taken down, but Immanuel's cemetery remains on the west side of Church Road.

In 1853, Henry Schmidt, a member of the Evangelical Zion Society of Leyden (a congregation distinct from the organization at Churchville; it met in a schoolhouse in Leyden Township), donated land at the corner of Church Road and Third Avenue for a church. A church was dedicated by Bishop John Seybert in 1854. In 1865, the building was moved to Cogswell Corner on Irving Park and Prospect. In 1874, the congregation built a new church on this location. In 1887, the congregation built a gothic frame church on Lincoln Street in Bensenville. This church was for many years a part of the Evangelical United Brethren denomination. A wind storm destroyed the top of the steeple in 1933. Rudy Laho recalls his father fashioned a new lightning rod apparatus, and Rudy himself climbed to the top of the steeple to install it. In 1967, the congregation built a new church on Church Road and is now the United Methodist Church of Bensenville.

PEACE CHURCH

Peace Church on Center Street was organized in 1903 by members of the Evangelical faith who lived in Bensenville, and who had attended St. John's or Immanuel. Afternoon services were originally held in the Gilde Hall at Green and Center. B. L. Franzen was the first president of the congregation, Herman H. Korthauer, the secretary, H. L. Geils, the finance secretary, and C. A. Franzen, the treasurer. A. D. Rotermund, Fred J. Mess, and W. F. Dunteman were the trustees. Nine lots were purchased on Center Street for $900 and the frame church built in 1903. The name of the church, Friedens Evangelical Church was chosen by ballot. Services and confirmation classes were conducted in German. In 1945, the name of the congregation was changed to Peace Evangelical and Reformed Church. The parsonage was dedicated in 1904. In 1956, a new educational building was finished and in 1968, the new sanctuary of Peace United Church of Christ was completed. The original frame church was torn down the same year.

Chain driven truck at the construction site of the second Immanuel Church, 1924

Present Immanuel Church, built in 1965

First Evangelical Church on Lincoln Street. Congregation moved to Church Road and became the United Methodist Church.

Building Frieden's Church in 1902   **133**

Frieden's Church 1902-1967

United Methodist Church

Present Peace Church on Center Street

St. Alexis Church, Wood and Rose Street, built in 1926

Interior of original St. Alexis Church

St. Alexis Church, Wood and Barron Street, celebrating its 50th Anniversary in 1976

Bensenville Community Church, Presbyterian, on Church Road

Bensenville Bible Church at York and Memorial

Bensenville's first Catholic Masses were said each Sunday at eight a.m., in the old village hall on York Road, beginning in 1921. Women of the parish set up the altar each Saturday night with linens, candles, vestments, and altar stone. A church was built in 1922 at the corner of Wood and Rose Streets, and dedicated by Archbishop Mundelein.

ST. ALEXIS The Rev. A. J. Milcheski became the first resident pastor in 1926, and the church became St. Alexis. The congregation outgrew the church, and on June 26, 1949, a new school was dedicated on Wood Street, on property that had been part of John Henry Franzen's homestead. The Sisters of St. Francis came to teach and live in quarters above the school. The sanctuary was in the basement of the school. The first pastor at the new school was Father Mathias Kauth. In 1957, the congregation moved from the school basement chapel into the new church, and in 1961, the convent was built to the east of the school.

BENSENVILLE BIBLE CHURCH Bensenville Bible Church worshipped for fifteen years in Frederick Wolkenhauer's gristmill on Center Street. The original group was part of a Bible study class that had met in Bensenville in the early 1900's. During the years it met at the mill, modifications were made in the building to accommodate Sunday School classes and church services. In 1950, a new church was built on York Road at Memorial.

BENSENVILLE COMMUNITY CHURCH Bensenville Community Church, Presbyterian, held its first worship service in November of 1954, in the band room of Tioga School. Conway E. Ramseyer was the first minister and organizing pastor. The congregation outgrew the band room and moved to the Little Theater at Fenton in 1955. A farm on Church Road was purchased the next year as the site for the church. A condition of the sale was that the crop could be harvested before ground was broken. The first worship service in the new church was held in September, 1958. The manse was finished that same year, and the educational wing completed in 1962.

St. Charles Borromeo Church was built in 1960 on Martin Luessenhop's farm to serve the developing Brentwood area south of Bensenville. Rev. Leonard Lenc was

St. Charles Borromeo Church

First Church of Christ Scientist on Church Road at Third Avenue

First Baptist Church on Foster at Highway 83

Grace Lutheran Church at 950 S. York Road

the founding pastor. On Christmas Eve, 1960, the first Mass was celebrated in the uncompleted church. The Sisters of St. Agnes arrived in August of 1961 to open the school, and by 1964, all eight grades were being taught. In 1964, the convent was built and the Luessenhop's farmhouse was renovated to become the rectory. In 1975, the church's fifteenth anniversary was celebrated by the blessing of the renovated sanctuary and the consecrating of a new altar.

ST. CHARLES
BORROMEO
CHURCH

The first Christian Science services were conducted by Edward Gallun and Mrs. Esther Wimsett in 1953 in the Milwaukee Railroad Women's Clubhouse. In 1966, a new church was completed on the southwest corner of Church Road and Third Avenue.

CHRISTIAN
SCIENCE
CHURCH

The Primera Iglesia Bautista (First Baptist Church) was begun in 1949, in a school in Des Plaines, and moved to Foster and Highway 83 in Bensenville in 1956, to serve the Spanish-speaking citizens. In 1976, a simultaneous interpreting system will provide the congregation a Spanish language translation of the English church service.

PRIMERA
IGLESIA
BAUTISTA

Calvary Baptist Church at 306 Park Street

St. Bede's Episcopal Church

Grace Lutheran Church was organized in 1960 by the Rev. Norman E. Benson. The church is located at 950 South York Road. Calvary Baptist Church, 306 Park Street, was organized in 1964 by Rev. Edward Ferrell.

St. Bede's Episcopal Church was established May 1, 1957. The congregation met first at Fenton High School under the charge of Rev. William Deutsch. On December 24, 1965, the new church was dedicated at 5N047 Route 83.

SOURCES

Bateman, Newton and Paul Selby, ed. *Historical Encyclopedia of Illinois*, and *History of DuPage County*, Volumes I and II. Chicago: Munsell, 1913.

Bates, Frederick. *Old Elmhurst*. Elmhurst Historical Commission, 1973.

Berens, Helmut Alan. *Elmhurst: Prairie to Tree Town*. Elmhurst Historical Commission, 1968.

The Bensenville Record. Vol. III No. 9. (May 3, 1895).

Bensenville Register. Paddock Publications, Inc.

Blanchard, Rufus. *History of DuPage County, Illinois*. Chicago: Baskin and Co., 1882.

Comprehensive Plan, Village of Bensenville. Chicago: Carl L. Gardner & Associates, Inc. 1963.

The Cradle of the Lutheran Church in Chicagoland: A Review of the History of Zion Church, Bensenville, Illinois. 1963.

50th Anniversary History of the Bensenville Volunteer Fire Department, 1944.

First Annual Bensenville Day, 1961.

Green Street School 50th Anniversary, 1966.

Johnson, Rita M. *History of Churchville School*, 1954.

Josephy, Alvin M. *The Indian Heritage of America*. Bantam, 1969.

Knoblauck, Marion, re-ed. 1948. *DuPage County, A Descriptive and Historical Guide*. American Guide Series, 1831-1939, compiled and written by the W.P.A.

Portrait and Biographical Record of DuPage and Cook Counties, Illinois. Chicago: Lake City Publishing Company, 1894.

60th Anniversary History of the Bensenville Volunteer Fire Department, 1954.

The Story of a Family. St. Alexis Church, Bensenville, Illinois, 1949.

Thompson Bros. and Burr. *New Combination Atlas, DuPage County, Illinois. 1874*.

UNPUBLISHED SOURCES

Barth, Victor C. "History of Immanuel Church, Bensenville, 1966."

Bensenville Community Public Library Records.

"History of Peace Church, 1968."

"History of the United Methodist Church of Bensenville, Illinois."

Johnson, Wesley A. "History of Elementary School District 2 and Green Street School."

Minutes of District 100 School Board Meetings.

Minutes of District 2 School Board Meetings.

Minute Books of the Milwaukee Railroad Woman's Club.

Northrop, Virginia. "Overview of the Development of the Bensenville Community Public Library."

St. John's Church 125th Anniversary Bulletin.

Tett, Walter. "History of the Bensenville Police Department."

Village of Bensenville Minute Books.

Wooley, Gertrude. "Story of Bensenville."

This book, *Bensenville*, has been published
in an edition of
three thousand five hundred copies.
Internal design and composition by
Graphic Arts Production, Itasca, Illinois.
Printing and binding by
NAPCO Graphics, New Berlin, Wisconsin.
Cover design by
George Korthauer, Jr. Bensenville.